Children
in the World

by

**Magda Cordell McHale
and John McHale
with
Guy F. Streatfeild**

Center for Integrative Studies
Library Building
University of Houston
Houston, Texas 77004 U.S.A.

A publication of the
POPULATION REFERENCE BUREAU
WASHINGTON, D.C. 20036 U.S.A.

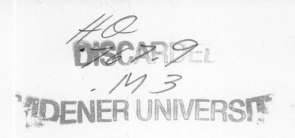
The authors wish to acknowledge those who worked with them in preparing this chartbook: Terri Phillips and Angela Gonzales, their colleagues at the Center for Integrative Studies, University of Houston, Texas; Jean van der Tak, Director of Publications, and Thomas T. Kane, Research Demographer, of the Population Reference Bureau; and Dr. Frances G. Conn, Consultant.

They are also grateful to those who made available invaluable material, particularly, Dr. Noel Brown, Chief of Liaison Office, and Gabrielle Gervais, Liaison Officer, of the United Nations Environment Programme; Dr. Ivan Schwarz, Chief of Documents, Reference and Collections, of the United Nations Dag Hammarskjöld Library; and Wadi D. Haddad, Education Department, Central Projects Staff, the World Bank; and for additional research, to Martha Sanford Munitz and Evan McHale.

Publication of this chartbook in observance of the International Year of the Child 1979 was made possible by a special grant from the U.S. Agency for International Development. The conclusions reached do not necessarily represent the views of the U.S. Government.

Published in 1979 by

Population Reference Bureau, Inc.
1337 Connecticut Avenue N.W.
Washington, D.C. 20036

Library of Congress Cataloging in Publication Data

McHale, Magda Cordell.
  Children in the world.

  1. Children – Statistics I. McHale, John, joint author, II. Title.
HQ767.9.M3   301.43'1   78-24731
ISBN 0-917136-03-9

Additional copies of *Children in the World* may be ordered from the Population Reference Bureau.

contents

The situation of the world's children, about 1975

There are 1,439 million children under the age of 15 in the world. Of these:

693 million	**(48%)**	will live less than 60 years.
5 million	**(0.3%)**	die each year from six major infectious diseases.
230 million	**(16%)**	are undernourished.
590 million	**(41%)**	are without access to safe water.
417 million	**(29%)**	are without adequate housing.
604 million	**(42%)**	are without access to effective medical care.
250 million		are of school age (5-14) and out of school – about 35% of that age group.
72 million	**(5%)**	suffer from severe handicaps.
173 million	**(12%)**	need special education or rehabilitation services.
396 million	**(27.5%)**	live in countries where average income per capita is less than $200 per year.
58 million	**(4%)**	are nomadic and semi-nomadic.
156 million	**(11%)**	live in slums and squatter settlements.
600 thousand	**(0.04%)**	are refugees.

The above figures are rough estimates, derived from a variety of sources.

introduction

The Population Reference Bureau is pleased to present this chartbook, *Children in the World,* in observance of the International Year of the Child 1979, proclaimed by the United Nations for advocacy and action on behalf of the world's children. The chartbook supplements the Population Bulletin *World of Children* and the *World's Children Data Sheet* by the same authors, also published by and available from the Bureau.

In 1975, more than one third of the world's some four billion people – close to one and a half billion – were children under the age of 15. By the year 2000, if current projections hold, there will be nearly two billion children in the world.

It is not the absolute numbers of children which are so important, however, though they are critical enough. It is their distribution throughout the world and their relative numbers in specific populations that makes the plight of most of the world's children an emergency.

About four of every five children in the world (80 percent) live in the less developed regions where in some countries they make up almost half of the population. By the year 2000, 84 percent will live in these areas. Most of the less developed countries are unable to feed, house, educate, and protect the health of all their children at even minimally adequate levels.

This chartbook documents the situation with the most current data now available, describing the disparities between life for the more fortunate fifth of the world's children and that of the other four fifths. Understanding the needs of children will provide the basis for planning and implementing programs and projects which will help ensure that every child born has the chance to realize his or her potential as a human being.

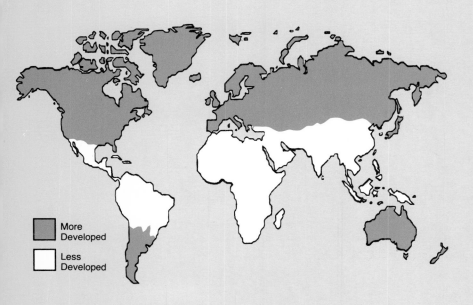

More Developed

Less Developed

The classification of "more developed" and "less developed" regions used in this chartbook follows that of the United Nations. "More developed" regions include all of Europe, Northern America (the United States, Canada, Greenland and Bermuda), Australia and New Zealand, Japan, the U.S.S.R., and Temperate South America (Argentina, Chile and Uruguay). The rest of the world is regarded as "less developed."

dimensions of childhood

Children do not vote and they do not have political parties, but their needs and rights have become part of the constituency of global concern. The realization of the centrality of the human in development extends to the overall development of children. They are no longer viewed merely as a kind of property, as new resources for, or burdens upon society's growth, nor as tools for its economic and other purposes – but are to be valued in and for themselves and for their hope, potential, and rights as human beings.

Childhood is a universal experience, marked by common needs and development. For most purposes in most societies today, this period covers the years under the age of 15. This is the age range targeted for the International Year of the Child and used generally throughout this chartbook, although some data are presented for the later teen years.

A useful conceptual framework for considering the needs and developmental requirements of the different stages of childhood is to view them within the overall life cycle. Although infancy and childhood occupy only a small fraction of the life span, they are the most crucial years in determining and influencing the course of adult life.

The needs of the child start with conception and pre-birth development. It is born helpless and totally dependent, but with a personal uniqueness and individuality – and vociferous demands for attention, care and security. Early physical development is rapid with greater changes in the first few years of life than at any subsequent stage. Psychosocial, intellectual and emotional development also expand more rapidly in these years than in any other period. After the relatively stable growth years of mid-childhood, the onset of puberty marks the physiological transition to adulthood. Considering the magnitude of these changes – in body weight, size, physical configuration, mental, emotional, and personality growth – infancy and childhood are like a whole life within a lifetime.

INTRAUTERINE
The period before birth

NEONATAL
First 4 weeks

INFANT
Ages 0-1

The stages of childhood

The stages of growth in childhood have been variously categorized. It is useful to have appropriate norms established for each stage so that a child's condition can be adequately evaluated; e.g., the age at which it might be expected to walk, reach a certain weight, or arrive at puberty, usually about age 12 for girls and age 14 for boys, although there is wide variation throughout the world.

Most of the charts in this chartbook were conceptualized and prepared by the Center for Integrative Studies, University of Houston, Houston, Texas.

PRESCHOOL
Ages 2-5

EARLY SCHOOL
Girls: Ages 6-9
Boys: Ages 6-11

PREPUBESCENT
Girls: Ages 10-11
Boys: Ages 12-13

ADOLESCENT
Girls: Ages 12-17
Boys: Ages 14-19

SOURCE: McHale, McHale, Streatfeild, *Population Bulletin,* January 1979

Stages of the life cycle

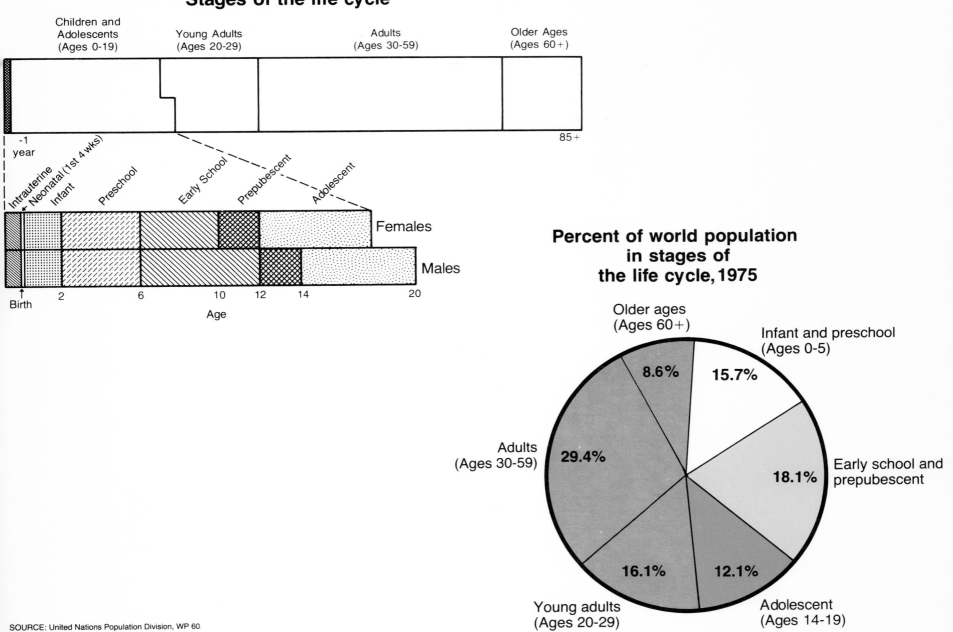

Children and Adolescents (Ages 0-19)

Young Adults (Ages 20-29)

Adults (Ages 30-59)

Older Ages (Ages 60+)

-1 year

85+

Intrauterine

Neonatal (1st 4 wks)

Infant

Preschool

Early School

Prepubescent

Adolescent

Females

Males

Birth

2 6 10 12 14 20

Age

Percent of world population in stages of the life cycle, 1975

Older ages (Ages 60+) 8.6%

Infant and preschool (Ages 0-5) 15.7%

Early school and prepubescent 18.1%

Adults (Ages 30-59) 29.4%

Adolescent (Ages 14-19) 12.1%

Young adults (Ages 20-29) 16.1%

SOURCE: United Nations Population Division, WP 60

how many children are there and where are they?

In 1975 there were just over 4 billion people in the world and 1.4 billion of them – 36 percent – were children under age 15. By the year 2000, if current projections hold, there will be 1.9 billion children in the world – 500 million more than in 1975.

Eighty percent of the world's children in 1975 – 1.2 billion – lived in the less developed regions where many countries lack sufficient resources to feed, clothe, house, educate and care for the health of their children – and to ensure jobs for them when they grow up.

As the world marks the International Year of the Child, about 334,000 babies are being born each day. In 1975, the annual birth rate ranged from 41 to 49 per 1,000 population in Africa; from 23 to 42 per 1,000 in Latin America; and from 22 to 40 per 1,000 in Asia. In Northern America (the United States and Canada), the birth rate was 15, and in Western Europe, just 11 per 1,000.

High birth rates lead to high proportions of young children in the population. In the less developed countries as a whole in 1975, children under 15 made up 40 percent of the total population compared to 25 percent in the more developed regions. In Africa the proportion of children was 44 percent, and in Latin America, 42 percent. A high proportion of dependent children is a heavy economic burden for the proportion of a country's people in the working ages (usually thought of as ages 15 to 64).

The proportion of children in the world's population is projected to fall to 32 percent in the year 2000 because birth rates have begun to fall in some less developed countries. However, the proportion will still be a high 34 percent in the less developed regions. In more developed countries the proportion of children will be 22 percent.

In 1975 about 800 million children under the age of 15 lived in the rural areas of the less developed countries. Despite the great ongoing migration to the cities, the number of rural children is growing rapidly. In these areas, birth rates and infant death rates are higher than in urban areas – in some cases twice as high. Less than 15 percent of the people live within walking distance of a health facility. Millions of children have no opportunity to attend school.

On the other hand, in 1975, there were some 156 million children in the less developed countries who were living in the slums and squatter settlements of the cities. These children live in overcrowded conditions, sharing a room with four, six or even ten other people. Their playground is a world of open sewers and garbage dumps in which disease is an ever-constant threat.

People living in slums and squatter settlements currently make up 30 to 40 percent of the urban population in less developed countries and are increasing in number faster than the overall urban population. Many cities in the less developed world, already hard pressed to service their burgeoning populations, are expected to triple or even quadruple their numbers between 1975 and the end of the century.

Proportion of children under age 15 in the world population, 1975

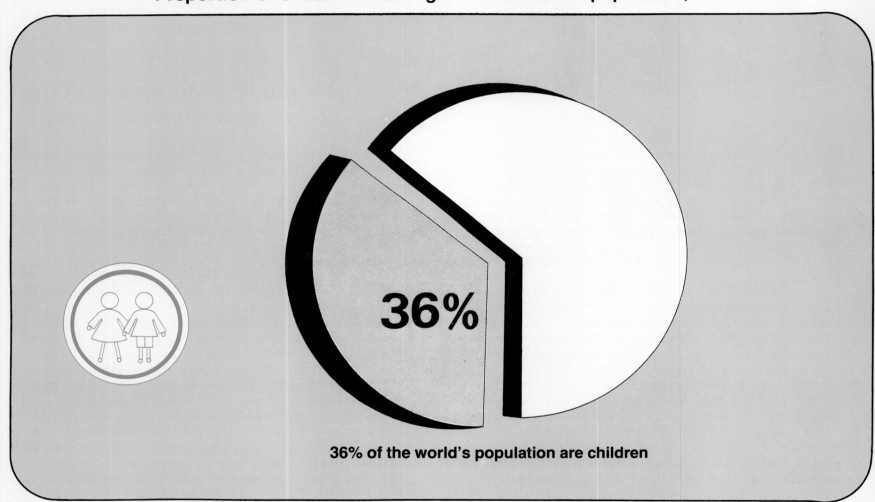

36%

36% of the world's population are children

SOURCE: Population Reference Bureau, *World's Children Data Sheet,* 1979

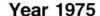

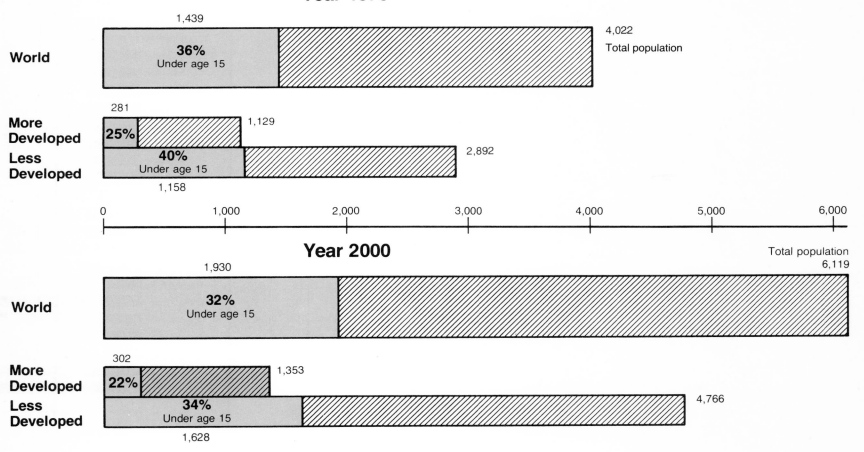

Number of children under age 15 and as percent of total population, world, more developed and less developed regions, 1975 and 2000

(Numbers in millions)

Year 1975

More developed regions include all Europe, the U.S.S.R., Japan, Northern America (the United States and Canada), Temperate South America (Argentina, Chile and Uruguay), Australia and New Zealand. Less developed regions include all other countries.

SOURCE: Population Reference Bureau, *World's Children Data Sheet*, 1979

Number of children under age 15 in more developed and less developed regions, 1975-2000

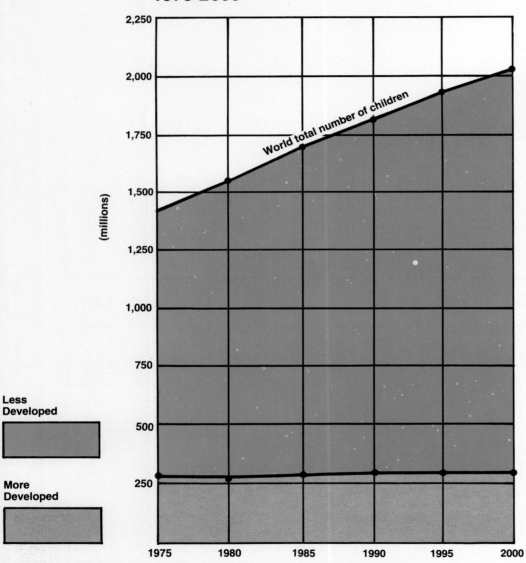

(millions)

2,250
2,000
1,750
1,500
1,250
1,000
750
500
250

World total number of children

Less Developed

More Developed

1975   1980   1985   1990   1995   2000

More developed regions include all Europe, the U.S.S.R., Japan, Northern America (the United States and Canada), Temperate South America (Argentina, Chile and Uruguay), Australia and New Zealand. Less developed regions include all other countries.

SOURCE: United Nations Population Division, WP 60

These data are based on United Nations projections prepared in 1973. The numbers of children for 1975 and 2000 differ slightly from those for the same years shown in the chart on page 13 and cited in the text which are based on more recent estimates and projections by the World Bank and the U.S. Bureau of the Census.

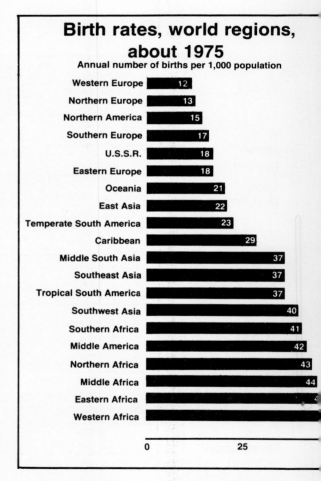

Birth rates, world regions, about 1975
Annual number of births per 1,000 population

Western Europe	12
Northern Europe	13
Northern America	15
Southern Europe	17
U.S.S.R.	18
Eastern Europe	18
Oceania	21
East Asia	22
Temperate South America	23
Caribbean	29
Middle South Asia	37
Southeast Asia	37
Tropical South America	37
Southwest Asia	40
Southern Africa	41
Middle America	42
Northern Africa	43
Middle Africa	44
Eastern Africa	
Western Africa	

0   25

SOURCE: Population Reference Bureau, *1978 World Population Data Sheet*

Number of children under age 15 and as percent of total population, world regions, 1975 and 2000
(Numbers in millions)

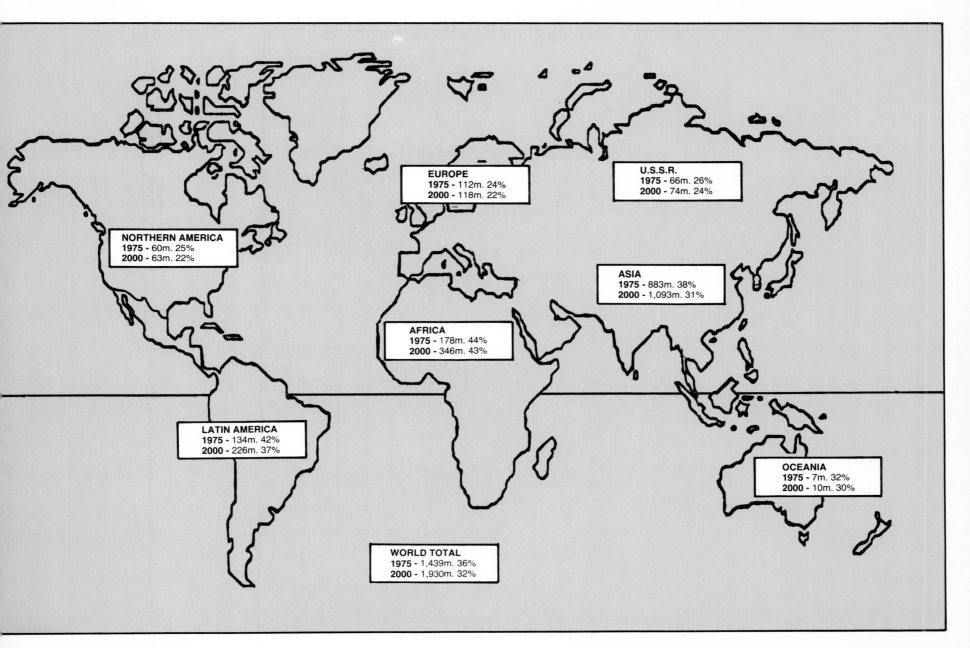

EUROPE
1975 - 112m. 24%
2000 - 118m. 22%

U.S.S.R.
1975 - 66m. 26%
2000 - 74m. 24%

NORTHERN AMERICA
1975 - 60m. 25%
2000 - 63m. 22%

ASIA
1975 - 883m. 38%
2000 - 1,093m. 31%

AFRICA
1975 - 178m. 44%
2000 - 346m. 43%

LATIN AMERICA
1975 - 134m. 42%
2000 - 226m. 37%

OCEANIA
1975 - 7m. 32%
2000 - 10m. 30%

WORLD TOTAL
1975 - 1,439m. 36%
2000 - 1,930m. 32%

RCE: Population Reference Bureau, *World's Children Data Sheet,* 1979.

Number of people in more developed and less developed regions of the world, by age and sex, 1975 and 2000

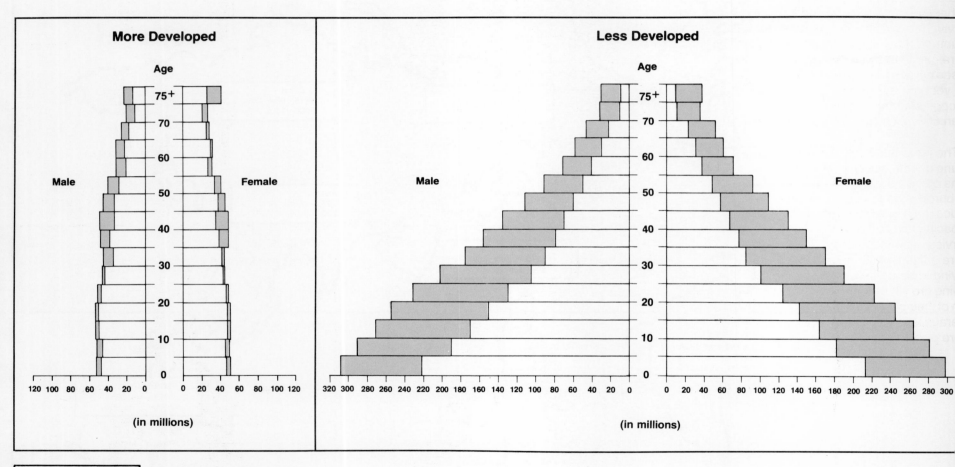

More Developed

Age

Male

Female

(in millions)

Less Developed

Age

Male

Female

(in millions)

population in 1975

increase 1975 to 2000

SOURCE: United Nations Population Division, WP 60

Number of people in United States, Japan, Brazil, and Bangladesh by age and sex, 1975 and 2000

Less developed countries tend to have higher birth rates and a lower chance of survival into old age than more developed countries. Their population distribution is therefore typically represented by a wide-based pyramid, with many more people in the younger age groups. The more developed countries show a much more even distribution among age cohorts.

The large numbers of children and young people being added to the populations of the poorer countries mean heavy burdens on their child-rearing and education resources in situations where capacities are already under strain. Services and resources in many of the more affluent countries, however, are having to deal with a zero or even declining growth rate of the younger proportion of their populations, an increase in the average age of their people, and relatively more people in the older age groups.

population in 1975

increase 1975 to 2000

decrease 1975 to 2000

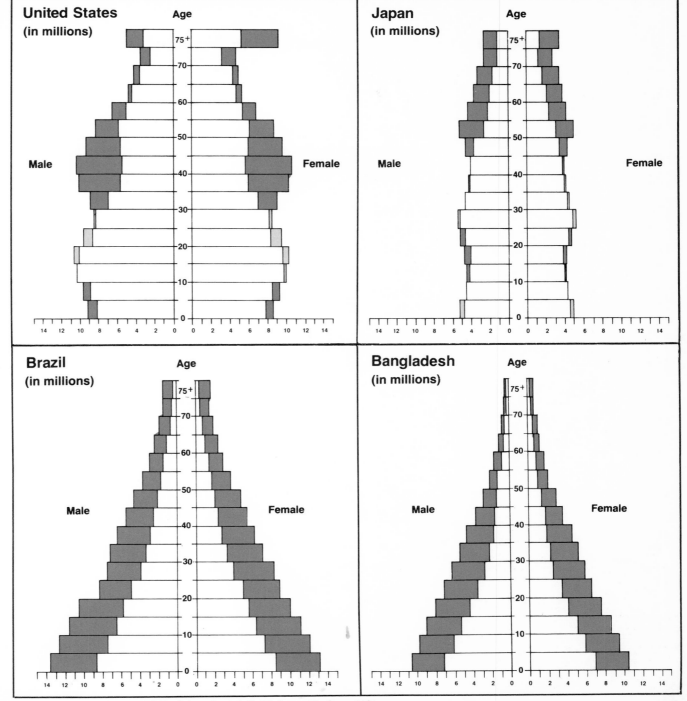

SOURCE: World Bank projections, 1978 (Brazil, Japan, Bangladesh); U.S. Bureau of the Census (U.S.)

Number of children under age 15 in urban and rural areas, world, selected regions, 1975, 1980, 1990, and 2000

(in millions)

		1975	1980	1990	2000
WORLD	URBAN	504	586	770	953
	RURAL	924	970	1,066	1,072
MORE DEVELOPED REGIONS	URBAN	195	204	234	249
	RURAL	88	79	70	58
LESS DEVELOPED REGIONS	URBAN	309	382	536	704
	RURAL	836	891	996	1,014
AFRICA	URBAN	42	55	87	133
	RURAL	135	149	186	217
LATIN AMERICA	URBAN	82	99	137	174
	RURAL	54	55	58	58
SOUTH ASIA	URBAN	124	152	226	290
	RURAL	415	457	527	539

These data are based on United Nations projections prepared in 1973. The total numbers of children for 1975 and 2000 differ slightly from those for the same years shown in earlier charts and cited in the text which are based on more recent estimates and projections by the World Bank and the U.S. Bureau of the Census.

In dividing countries' populations into "urban" and "rural," the United Nations follows the definitions of individual countries. These can vary widely. For example, the minimum number of inhabitants needed to classify a place as "urban" can range from as few as 200 people (Denmark) to as many as 50,000 (Japan).

SOURCE: United Nations Population Division, WP 54

Percentage population
increase in world's fastest growing cities, 1976-1986

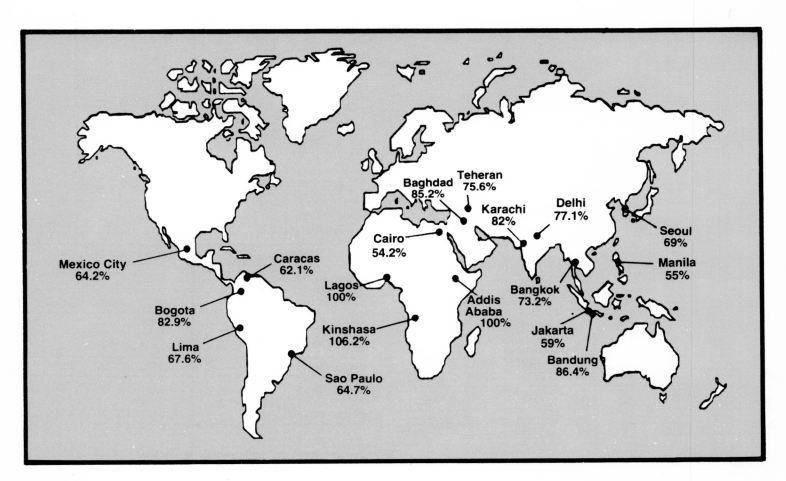

Baghdad 85.2%
Teheran 75.6%
Karachi 82%
Delhi 77.1%
Seoul 69%
Cairo 54.2%
Manila 55%
Mexico City 64.2%
Caracas 62.1%
Lagos 100%
Bangkok 73.2%
Bogota 82.9%
Addis Ababa 100%
Jakarta 59%
Lima 67.6%
Kinshasa 106.2%
Bandung 86.4%
Sao Paulo 64.7%

SOURCE: *Development Forum*, January/February, 1976

Total population in selected cities, 1950, 1975, and 2000

(in thousands)

Africa	1950	1975	% increase 1950-1975	2000	% increase 1975-2000
Cairo (Egypt)	2,377	6,932	(192%)	16,398	(137%)
Lagos (Nigeria)	288	2,064	(617%)	9,437	(357%)
Kinshasa (Zaire)	164	2,049	(1149%)	9,112	(345%)

Latin America					
Mexico City (Mexico)	2,872	10,942	(281%)	31,616	(189%)
Sao Paulo (Brazil)	2,450	9,965	(307%)	26,045	(161%)
Lima (Peru)	614	3,901	(535%)	12,130	(211%)

Asia	1950	1975	% increase 1950-1975	2000	% increase 1975-2000
Calcutta (India)	4,446	8,077	(81%)	19,633	(143%)
Jakarta (Indonesia)	1,565	5,593	(257%)	16,933	(203%)
Teheran (Iran)	1,041	4,435	(326%)	13,785	(211%)

Europe					
Paris (France)	5,441	9,189	(69%)	12,293	(34%)
Milan (Italy)	3,641	6,030	(66%)	8,267	(37%)
London (U.K.)	10,247	10,711	(5%)	12,693	(19%)

Other Industrialized Countries					
Moscow (U.S.S.R.)	4,841	7,609	(57%)	10,623	(40%)
Tokyo-Yokohama (Japan)	6,737	17,317	(157%)	26,128	(51%)
New York-N.E. New Jersey (U.S.)	12,340	17,013	(38%)	22,212	(31%)

SOURCE: United Nations Population Division, WP 58

Growth rates of urban population, slums, and squatter settlements; selected countries, various years

annual growth rates by percent

LATIN AMERICA		urban population	slum and squatter population
Brazil			
Rio de Janeiro	1970	4.4	5.5
Colombia			
Buenaventura	1969	0.4	0.4
Cali		7.4	7.4
Guatemala			
Guatemala City	1971	5.3	28.0
Honduras			
Tegucigalpa	1970	5.2	5.2
Mexico			
Mexico City	1966	2.3	12.0
Panama			
Panama City	1970	5.9	5.9
Peru			
Arequipa	1961	3.5	50.0
Chimbote	1961	5.0	60.0
Lima	1971	5.9	13.7
Venezuela			
Caracas	1974	4.5	5.7
Ciudad Guayana	1969	13.7	13.7
Maracaibo		7.2	7.2

EAST ASIA		urban population	slum and squatter population
South Korea			
Pusan	1969	3.7	32.2
Seoul	1966	6.7	56.6

SOUTH ASIA		urban population	slum and squatter population
Kampuchea			
Phnom Penh	1972	10.4	16.4
India			
Bombay	1971	3.6	17.4
Calcutta	1971	2.5	9.1
Indonesia			
Jakarta	1972	4.2	4.6
Jordan			
Amman	1972	9.5	19.1
Malaysia			
Kuala Lumpur	1969	2.5	8.0
Pakistan			
Karachi	1971	5.6	10.0
Philippines			
Manila	1972	4.0	5.5
Turkey			
Total	1971	4.9	7.0
Ankara	1970	5.0	9.5
Istanbul	1970	6.5	11.6

AFRICA		urban population	slum and squatter population
Ghana			
Total	1970	4.6	17.5
Kenya			
Nairobi	1970	10.0	22.5
Morocco			
Total	1971	5.3	7.0
Tanzania			
Dar es Salaam	1970	7.0	35.7
Zambia			
Lusaka	1969	12.0	45.0

SOURCE: United Nations, ECOSOC, 1976

Average number of persons per household,
selected cities in more developed and less developed regions, various years

Cities in less developed regions	
Cairo (1966)	5.0
Nairobi (1969)	4.3
Lusaka (1969)	4.7
Santa Domingo (1970)	5.1
Kingston (1970)	3.6
Mexico City (1970)	5.0
Buenos Aires (1970)	3.1
Bogota (1973)	5.7
Hong Kong (1971)	4.5
New Delhi (1971)	5.0
Amman (1971)	6.5
Seoul (1970)	5.0
Singapore (1970)	5.3
Bangkok (1970)	6.1
Average	4.9

Cities in more developed regions	
Tokyo (1970)	3.1
Vienna (1970)	2.2
Sofia (1965)	2.8
Prague (1970)	2.5
Helsinki (1970)	2.5
Paris (1968)	2.6
West Berlin (1971)	2.4
Athens (1971)	3.1
Budapest (1970)	2.5
Dublin (1971)	3.9
Rome (1971)	3.3
Oslo (1970)	2.6
Warsaw (1970)	2.7
London (1971)	3.1
Average	2.8

SOURCE: United Nations Department of Economic and Social Affairs, 1976.

Children in rural areas of the poorest countries, 1975

A vast proportion of the world's children live in rural areas of the 68 poorest countries where the average income per person is less than $500 per year.

In 28 countries where the average income is $200 or less per person, there are:

959,059,000 people.
772,612,000 of them (81%) live in rural areas.
316,771,000 of these rural people (41%) are under age 15.

In 40 countries where the average annual income is between $200 and $500 per person, there are:

1,355,929,000 people.
1,034,405,000 of them (76%) live in rural areas.
382,730,000 of these rural people (37%) are under age 15.

SOURCES: *World Bank Atlas,* 1978; Population Reference Bureau, *1978 World Population Data Sheet*

who are they?

Children are male, female, sons, daughters, brothers and sisters, and some are parents – 10 to 15 percent of births worldwide are to teenagers.

Children are rich, poor; settled and nomadic. They belong to various ethnic and national groups, and grow up within different social, cultural, and religious traditions.

Of the 1.4 billion world's children under age 15 in 1975, 51 percent were boys and 49 percent, girls. A child's sex determines much about his or her life: for example, girls can expect to live longer than boys. In almost all countries, the death rate for males exceeds that of females from the moment of conception and continuing through life.

Children of the world speak one or more of about 3,000 different languages. Of every 100 children, about 19 speak Chinese (Mandarin, Cantonese, or another language of this group); about seven speak English; six speak Hindi; and slightly fewer speak Spanish.

Most children are brought up within some religious tradition, usually one related to one or another of the major world religions, chiefly Christian, Muslim (Islam), Hindu or Buddhist.

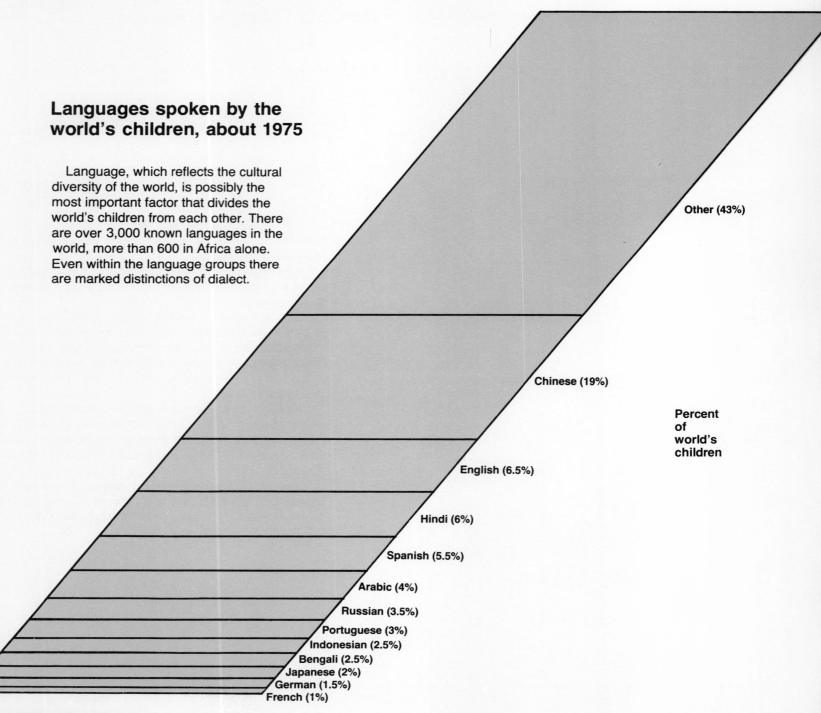

Languages spoken by the world's children, about 1975

Language, which reflects the cultural diversity of the world, is possibly the most important factor that divides the world's children from each other. There are over 3,000 known languages in the world, more than 600 in Africa alone. Even within the language groups there are marked distinctions of dialect.

Other (43%)

Chinese (19%)

Percent of world's children

English (6.5%)

Hindi (6%)

Spanish (5.5%)

Arabic (4%)

Russian (3.5%)

Portuguese (3%)

Indonesian (2.5%)

Bengali (2.5%)

Japanese (2%)

German (1.5%)

French (1%)

SOURCE: Adapted from *Rand McNally's Concise Atlas of the Earth*, 1976

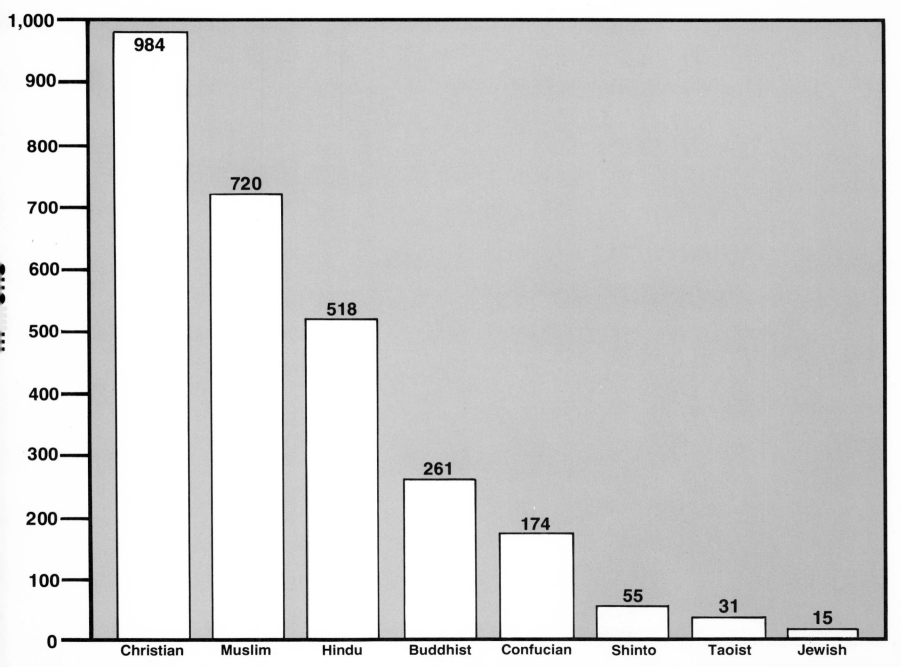

Estimated number of people affiliated with world's major religions, about 1975

(in millions)

Christian	984
Muslim	720
Hindu	518
Buddhist	261
Confucian	174
Shinto	55
Taoist	31
Jewish	15

SOURCE: *Britannica Book of the Year, 1978*; estimates for Muslims from Weekes (ed.), *Muslim Peoples: A World Ethnographic Survey, 1978*

how well do they live?

Selected development indicators by continent, about 1975

	Life expectancy at birth (years)	Infant mortality (per 1,000 live births)	Birth rate (per 1,000 pop.)	Death rate (per 1,000 pop.)	% of calorie requirements met	% urban (of total pop.)	Physicians (per 10,000 pop.)	Nursing and midwifery personnel (per 10,000 pop.)	Hospital beds (per 10,000 pop.)	Literacy rate (% of adult pop.)	Public expenditures on education per capita (U.S.$)	GNP per capita (U.S.$)	Energy consumption per capita (in kilograms of coal equivalent)	% enrolled in school, ages 6-11	% enrolled in school, ages 12-17
World	60	99	29	12	107	39	8.8	22.7	46.1	73	69	1,650	1,984	70	50
Northern America	73	15	15	9	134	74	16.5	63.6	75.2	99	389	7,850	11,526	99	95
Europe	71	20	15	10	130	65	16.6	37.5	93.6	97	166	4,420	4,125	96	80
U.S.S.R.	69	28	18	9	136	62	29.7	59.8	116.4	99	166	2,760	4,767	99	80
Oceania	68	41	21	9	127	71	11.0	31.1	101.7	98	274	4,730	4,275	88	73
Latin America	62	84	36	9	107	61	7.3	7.4	30.5	74	30	1,100	916	78	56
Asia	58	105	30	12	97	26	3.1	7.5	18.7	67	14	610	495	64	36
Africa	46	147	46	19	91	25	1.1	7.0	19.4	22	14	440	363	51	31

These figures give an overall impression of the disparities in social and economic conditions which govern the lives of the world's children.

health and disease

A child's chances for living and dying are very much affected by the social and economic conditions into which he or she is born.

In Africa as a whole, of every 1,000 children born, 147 die before reaching their first birthday, and the average newborn can expect to live only 46 years. In Europe, by contrast, of every 1,000 born, 20 die in the first year of life, and the average newborn can expect to live 71 years.

Though much more needs to be done, health conditions are now better for the world's children than they were in the past, and more are surviving longer. In 1900, in the least developed countries, nearly 265 of every 1,000 children born alive died before completing their first year, compared to about 75 in the more developed countries. By the mid-1970s, in the less developed countries as a whole, annual infant deaths in the first year of life had been reduced to an estimated 113 per 1,000 live births and in the more developed, to 22.

In the late 1930s, life expectancy at birth in the less developed regions was about 32 years – similar to what it was during Roman Empire times. Now it has increased to an estimated 56 years in the less developed regions as a whole and 71 years in the more developed regions.

Of the some 50 million deaths in the world each year, about a quarter occur to infants under age one, and about half to children under age five. Most of these deaths occur in the poorer countries of Africa, Asia, and Latin America. Millions of deaths are caused by such diseases as dysentery, typhoid, cholera, and pneumonia to which small children in poorer countries are particularly vulnerable. Five million children in the less developed countries die every year from six infectious diseases: diphtheria, whooping cough, poliomyelitis (infantile paralysis), measles, tetanus, and tuberculosis. Most, or perhaps all of these deaths could be prevented by immunizations which protect most children in the developed countries. The relatively fewer deaths which occur to infants and children in the more developed countries are more likely to result from causes that are less preventable such as accidents and birth defects.

In the least developed countries there is a vicious circle of social and economic deprivation which affects the health of children and adults alike and from which it is difficult to escape. Poor nutrition lowers resistance to disease. Hunger and ill health impair productivity, and this in turn lowers the capacity to secure food and improve living conditions which would help build resistance to disease. Inadequate housing, poor water sanitation, and unsanitary sewage disposal also contribute to high infant and child mortality, particularly from diarrheal diseases. High rates of child loss in turn encourage more childbearing which adds mouths to feed for which there is insufficient food, and more persons to clothe and shelter, for which there are insufficient resources.

A trend toward increasing substitution of bottled formulas for mother's breast milk in areas where clean water and adequate family incomes are lacking is associated with higher infant mortality from diarrhea and lowered disease resistance among infants and young children.

In the less developed countries and increasingly in the more developed countries, large numbers of children are born to mothers under age 20 – estimated at 10 to 15 percent of the some 122 million births worldwide each year. Babies born to adolescent girls face much higher risks of death and poor development than do those born to mothers in their twenties.

Infant mortality rates, world regions, about 1975

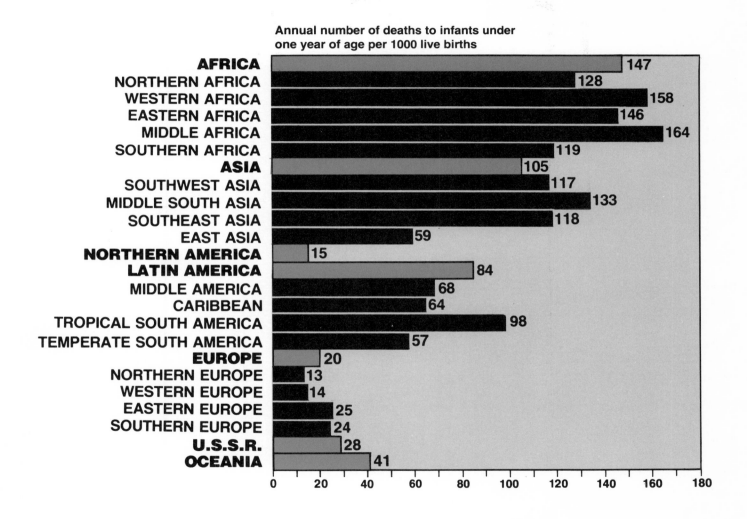

Annual number of deaths to infants under one year of age per 1000 live births

Region	Rate
AFRICA	147
NORTHERN AFRICA	128
WESTERN AFRICA	158
EASTERN AFRICA	146
MIDDLE AFRICA	164
SOUTHERN AFRICA	119
ASIA	105
SOUTHWEST ASIA	117
MIDDLE SOUTH ASIA	133
SOUTHEAST ASIA	118
EAST ASIA	59
NORTHERN AMERICA	15
LATIN AMERICA	84
MIDDLE AMERICA	68
CARIBBEAN	64
TROPICAL SOUTH AMERICA	98
TEMPERATE SOUTH AMERICA	57
EUROPE	20
NORTHERN EUROPE	13
WESTERN EUROPE	14
EASTERN EUROPE	25
SOUTHERN EUROPE	24
U.S.S.R.	28
OCEANIA	41

SOURCE: Population Reference Bureau, *1978 World Population Data Sheet*

Infant mortality rates, selected more developed countries, 1965-1975

The low infant death rates of affluent countries continue to fall, reaching under 9 per 1,000 live births in Sweden in recent years. By contrast, the rate in many African countries is still over 150.

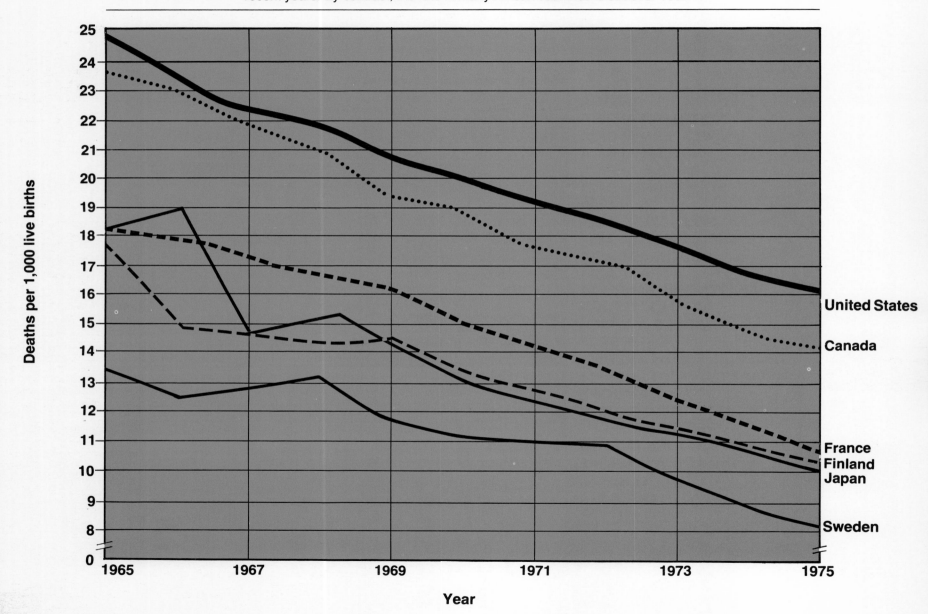

Deaths per 1,000 live births

Year

United States
Canada
France
Finland
Japan
Sweden

SOURCE: United Nations Statistical Office

Death rates at ages 1-4, selected countries in world regions, various years

In the less developed countries, children aged 1-4 still face relatively high risks of dying from diseases caused by malnutrition, poor sanitation, and lack of medical services. In most developed countries, only one child or fewer per 1,000 of those aged 1-4 dies per year.

AFRICA

	Annual deaths per 1,000 aged 1-4
Madagascar	33.3
Congo	30.0
Egypt	24.9
Benin	45.0
Togo	45.0

ASIA

	Annual deaths per 1,000 aged 1-4
Philippines	7.5
Afghanistan	24.1
Sri Lanka	3.8
Thailand	3.7
Turkey	14.6

LATIN AMERICA

	Annual deaths per 1,000 aged 1-4
Trinidad and Tobago	1.7
Mexico	4.6
Brazil	11.5
Ecuador	13.7
Venezuela	4.0

EUROPE

	Annual deaths per 1,000 aged 1-4
Czechoslovakia	0.9
Denmark	0.6
Greece	0.8
Portugal	1.9
Netherlands	0.7

U.S.S.R. & U.S.A.

	Annual deaths per 1,000 aged 1-4
U.S.S.R.	0.7
U.S.A.	0.8

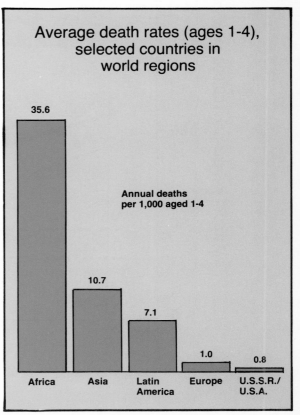

Average death rates (ages 1-4), selected countries in world regions

Annual deaths per 1,000 aged 1-4

Africa 35.6, Asia 10.7, Latin America 7.1, Europe 1.0, U.S.S.R./U.S.A. 0.8

URCE: World Health Organization, *Statistics Annual,* 1977; United Nations, *Demographic Yearbook,* 1976

Death rates at ages 5-14, selected countries, 1955-1975

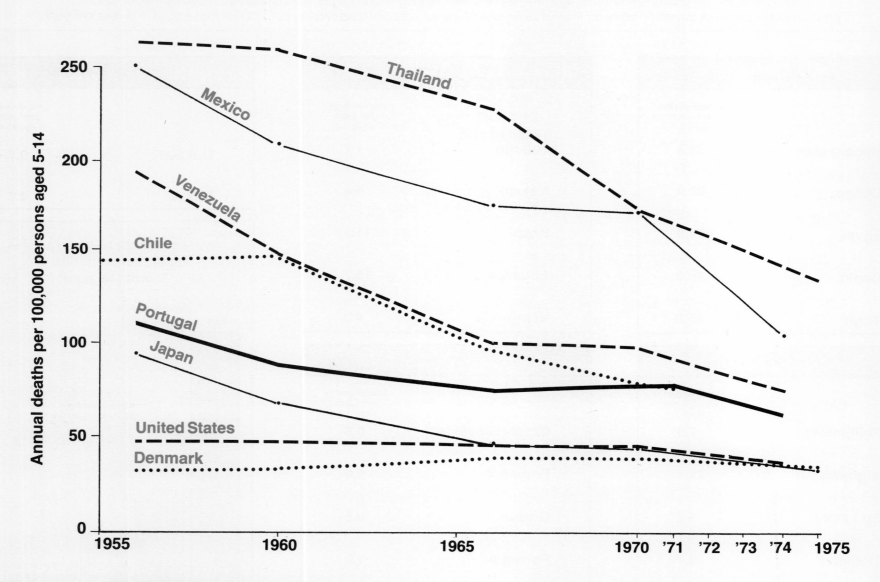

Annual deaths per 100,000 persons aged 5-14

Thailand

Mexico

Venezuela

Chile

Portugal

Japan

United States

Denmark

250

200

150

100

50

0

1955 1960 1965 1970 '71 '72 '73 '74 1975

SOURCE: World Health Organization, *Statistics Annual*, 1956-1977

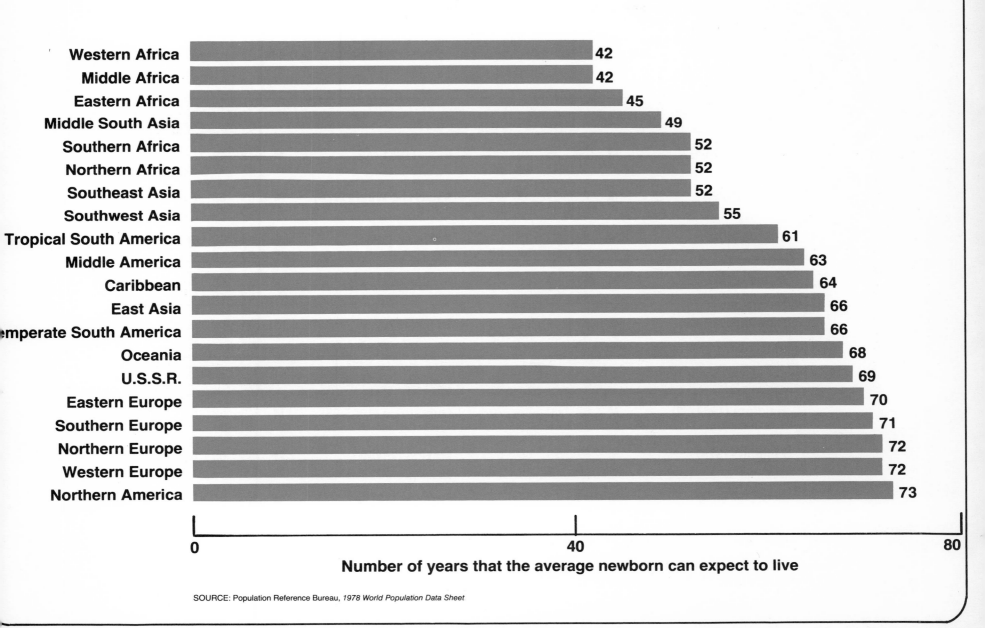

Life expectancy at birth, world regions, about 1976

Region	Years
Western Africa	42
Middle Africa	42
Eastern Africa	45
Middle South Asia	49
Southern Africa	52
Northern Africa	52
Southeast Asia	52
Southwest Asia	55
Tropical South America	61
Middle America	63
Caribbean	64
East Asia	66
Temperate South America	66
Oceania	68
U.S.S.R.	69
Eastern Europe	70
Southern Europe	71
Northern Europe	72
Western Europe	72
Northern America	73

0   40   80

Number of years that the average newborn can expect to live

SOURCE: Population Reference Bureau, *1978 World Population Data Sheet*

Average age at death for males and females surviving birth and reaching ages 1, 5, and 20, selected countries in world regions, various years

Low life expectancies in the less developed countries are partly due to high infant death rates. For example, in Malawi in the early 1970s, a boy's life expectancy at birth was just 41 years, but if he survived to age one, he could expect, on the average, to live to 49 years. In the more developed countries, average life expectancy is about the same at older ages as it is at birth. In nearly all countries, females have a higher life expectancy than males. The exceptions on this chart are India and Pakistan.

AFRICA		Age 0	1	5	20
Chad (1963-64)	M	29	35	39	46
	F	35	41	45	52
Kenya (1969)	M	47	54	59	63
	F	51	58	62	66
Liberia (1971)	M	46	53	57	61
	F	44	54	59	63
Malawi (1970-72)	M	41	49	66	72
	F	44	50	63	75
Nigeria (1965-66)	M	37	46	54	59
	F	37	44	52	58

ASIA		Age 0	1	5	20
India (1951-60)	M	42	49	54	57
	F	41	47	52	56
Malaysia, West (1974)	M	65	68	69	69
	F	70	73	73	74
Pakistan (1962)	M	54	62	66	68
	F	49	55	60	63
Sri Lanka (1967)	M	65	68	70	71
	F	67	70	72	73
Syria (1970)	M	54	62	66	67
	F	59	65	69	71

EUROPE		Age 0	1	5	20
Belgium (1968-72)	M	68	69	70	70
	F	74	76	76	76
Finland (1974)	M	67	68	68	69
	F	75	76	76	77
Italy (1970-72)	M	69	71	71	72
	F	75	77	77	77
Sweden (1971-75)	M	72	73	73	74
	F	78	78	78	79
Yugoslavia (1970-72)	M	65	69	70	70
	F	70	74	74	75

LATIN AMERICA		Age 0	1	5	20
Guatemala (1963-65)	M	48	53	59	63
	F	50	54	60	66
Mexico (1975)	M	63	69	69	70
	F	67	70	72	73
Panama (1970)	M	64	67	69	71
	F	68	70	72	74
Brazil (1960-70)	M	58	–	66	67
	F	61	–	68	70
Chile (1969-70)	M	60	66	66	67
	F	66	71	72	73

SOURCE: United Nations, *Demographic Yearbook*, 1976

Average age at death for people surviving birth and reaching ages 1, 5, 10, 15, and 20, selected countries, various years

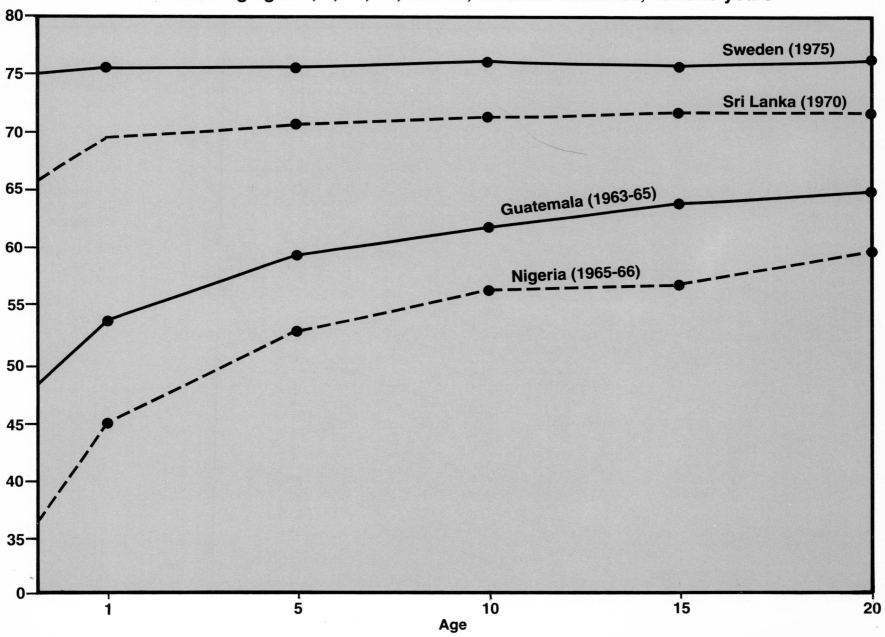

SOURCE: United Nations, *Demographic Yearbook,* 1976.

Trends in life expectancy, selected countries, 1850-1975

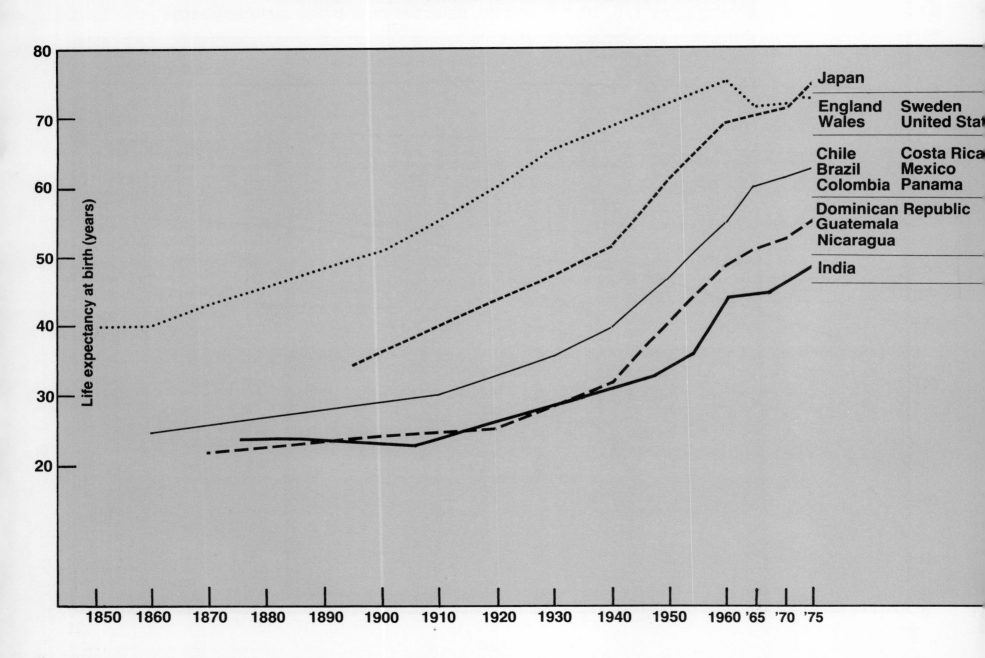

Life expectancy at birth (years)

Japan

England Wales   Sweden United Stat

Chile   Costa Rica
Brazil   Mexico
Colombia   Panama

Dominican Republic
Guatemala
Nicaragua

India

1850 1860 1870 1880 1890 1900 1910 1920 1930 1940 1950 1960 '65 '70 '75

SOURCES: Arriaga and Davis, *Demography,* Vol. 6, No. 2, 1969; United Nations Population Division, WP 65

mparison of major causes of children's deaths, selected countries, out 1975

the less developed countries, a large portion of children's deaths are due to asitic (causing diarrhea) and infec-s diseases (e.g., measles), and to ases of the respiratory system (e.g., nd pneumonia). Such diseases, once espread in the more developed coun-s, are now to a great extent averted by er nutrition, improved living condi-s, extensive clean water supply, age treatment, and preventive dical care such as immunization. The dren's deaths which do occur in the e developed countries are now more y to be due to less preventable cir-nstances such as accidents and birth ects (congenital anomalies).

0-1 years old
1-4 years old
5-14 years old

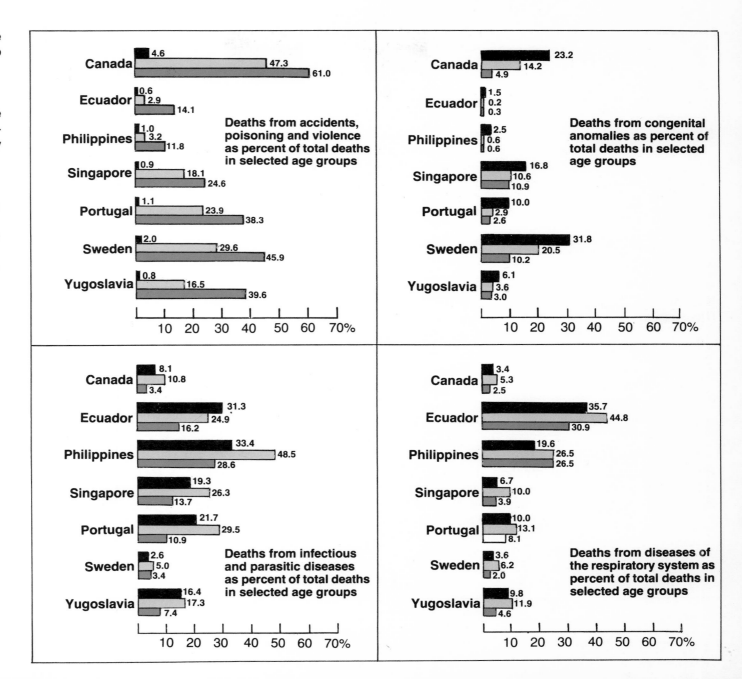

Deaths from accidents, poisoning and violence as percent of total deaths in selected age groups

Canada 4.6 / 47.3 / 61.0
Ecuador 0.6 / 2.9 / 14.1
Philippines 1.0 / 3.2 / 11.8
Singapore 0.9 / 18.1 / 24.6
Portugal 1.1 / 23.9 / 38.3
Sweden 2.0 / 29.6 / 45.9
Yugoslavia 0.8 / 16.5 / 39.6

Deaths from congenital anomalies as percent of total deaths in selected age groups

Canada 23.2 / 14.2 / 4.9
Ecuador 1.5 / 0.2 / 0.3
Philippines 2.5 / 0.6 / 0.6
Singapore 16.8 / 10.6 / 10.9
Portugal 10.0 / 2.9 / 2.6
Sweden 31.8 / 20.5 / 10.2
Yugoslavia 6.1 / 3.6 / 3.0

Deaths from infectious and parasitic diseases as percent of total deaths in selected age groups

Canada 8.1 / 10.8 / 3.4
Ecuador 31.3 / 24.9 / 16.2
Philippines 33.4 / 48.5 / 28.6
Singapore 19.3 / 26.3 / 13.7
Portugal 21.7 / 29.5 / 10.9
Sweden 2.6 / 5.0 / 3.4
Yugoslavia 16.4 / 17.3 / 7.4

Deaths from diseases of the respiratory system as percent of total deaths in selected age groups

Canada 3.4 / 5.3 / 2.5
Ecuador 35.7 / 44.8 / 30.9
Philippines 19.6 / 26.5 / 26.5
Singapore 6.7 / 10.0 / 3.9
Portugal 10.0 / 13.1 / 8.1
Sweden 3.6 / 6.2 / 2.0
Yugoslavia 9.8 / 11.9 / 4.6

RCE: World Health Organization, *Statistics Annual,* 1977

Six major infectious diseases which account for five million deaths of children under age 15 in the less developed countries each year

DISEASE	CAUSAL FACTORS	DESCRIPTION AND SYMPTOMS	PREVALENCE	PREVENTION AND TREATMENT
Diphtheria	A bacterial disease spread by contact with carriers who may appear healthy. Infected milk has occasionally been a vehicle for transmission of the disease.	Death occurs to 5-10% of affected persons. Tonsils, nose and throat most often infected, but heart and nerves may also be involved which may lead to heart failure, paralysis and sometimes death. Symptoms: sore throat, fever, or may be no symptoms.	Mainly in temperate regions in colder months. Primarily affects non-immunized children and adolescents. Effectively eliminated in more developed countries by use of vaccines.	Widescale immunization prevents the disease. Antitoxin and antibiotics for those contracting the disease.
Whooping Cough (Pertussis)	A bacterial disease transmitted via contact with nasal and throat secretions of infected persons.	Respiratory infection with characteristic cough, lasting 4-8 weeks. Young infants often do not have the typical cough. Serious complications include pneumonia, suffocation, and occasionally convulsions. More than one third of deaths occur to infants under five months.	Exists worldwide. In non-immunized populations, whooping cough is among the most serious of childhood diseases. Marked fall in incidence since the 1950s as a result of immunization and improved living conditions.	In most cases, can be prevented by immunization. Treatment for victims is with antibiotics and supportive measures.
Poliomyelitis (Polio, Infantile Paralysis)	Viral infection, may occur in epidemics. Usually transmitted via feces and throat secretions of infected persons, but infected milk has occasionally spread the disease.	Symptoms range from mild non-paralytic infection to extensive muscle paralysis including muscles used for breathing and swallowing which may cause death. More than 80% of patients recover without paralysis.	Before the use of vaccines, this disease affected millions, particularly children under age ten. Widespread immunization has resulted in a marked reduction in incidence.	Controlled by vaccination in more developed countries, capital cities of less developed countries since the 1960s.

Vaccines are available for the prevention of all six of these dangerous diseases. Improved standards of living (less crowding, better sanitation) plus widespread immunization of the population are crucial in their eradication.

EASE	CAUSAL FACTORS	DESCRIPTION AND SYMPTOMS	PREVALENCE	PREVENTION AND TREATMENT
sles beola)	Highly communicable viral infection spread by contact with nasal and throat secretions of infected persons. Community outbreaks take place every 2-4 years.	Fever and symptoms similar to severe cold, plus rash. Serious neurological complications and secondary bacterial infections of lungs may occur which may cause death. In some countries, more than half the blindness in childhood is due to measles. The disease is made more serious by malnutrition, particularly Vitamin A deficiency.	Exists worldwide. Measles is the infection which causes most deaths in many countries. Among malnourished children in less developed areas, death rate is 400 times that in more developed countries.	Live, attenuated vaccine produces immunity in more than 95% of children receiving it. There is no drug for treating measles once it has occurred.
anus ckjaw)	Caused by the toxin produced by the tetanus bacillus (a kind of bacteria). Introduced into the body through any kind of wound (even minor) or burn, usually by contact with dirt or animal feces which harbor the bacteria. Sometimes affects babies whose umbilical cord has been cut under non-sterile conditions.	Localized and generalized muscle spasms and convulsive seizures. Without immunization, the disease is fatal in 35-70% of cases.	More common in less developed countries where immunization programs are inadequate, where contact with animal feces is more common and where non-sterile childbirth techniques exist, e.g., putting animal dung on severed umbilical cord.	Routine immunization for prevention. Tetanus immuno-globulin (human) or antitoxin (animal) plus antibiotics (penicillin) for treatment of penetrating injury if patient has not received prior immunization. Sterile childbirth technique is important for preventing tetanus in newborn children.
erculosis	Transmitted via the sputum of infected individuals. Unpasteurized milk may act as a vehicle for TB from infected cows.	Principally a lung disease, but may progress to involve organs throughout the body. Symptoms include fever, cough, coughing up blood, weight loss, and fatigue, or there may be no symptoms. Disease may be detected by chest X-ray.	Worldwide, particularly where living conditions are crowded. Chief cause of death in many countries. Incidence has declined in the 20th century, primarily due to improved living standards.	Improved standard of living (less crowding) decreases the risk of infection. Vaccination with BCG in endemic areas (effectiveness of BCG is unknown). Mild pasteurization. Routine chest X-ray and skin testing of population for detecting exposed individuals. Antibiotic treatment for persons with active disease.

Number of people per physician, nurse/midwife, and hospital bed, world regions, about 1975

Regions	Population per physician*	Population per nurse/midwife**	Population per hospital bed*
World	1,363	564	260
Africa	9,091	1,429	515
Northern America	606	157	133
Latin America	1,370	1,351	328
Asia	9,091	1,429	515
Europe	602	267	107
Oceania	909	322	98
U.S.S.R.	337	167	86

*Excluding People's Republic of China, North Korea, Vietnam, Bhutan, and Sikkim.
**For countries with 2,408 million (62% of world population).

health personnel and facilities

It is the exception rather than the rule for children in the less developed countries to have access to the professional services of a nurse or midwife, let alone a qualified physician. In Asia, for example, 7 out of 10 infants are born without medical assistance or trained help.

The overall ratio of children to professional health personnel, bad as it is, masks the situation within countries where rural people are even more poorly served. Fewer than 15 percent of rural people in less developed countries live within walking distance of any kind of health facility.

SOURCE: World Health Organization, *Statistics Annual*, 1977; United Nations *Statistical Yearbook*, 1976

Number of people per physician, nurse/midwife, and hospital bed, selected countries, about 1975

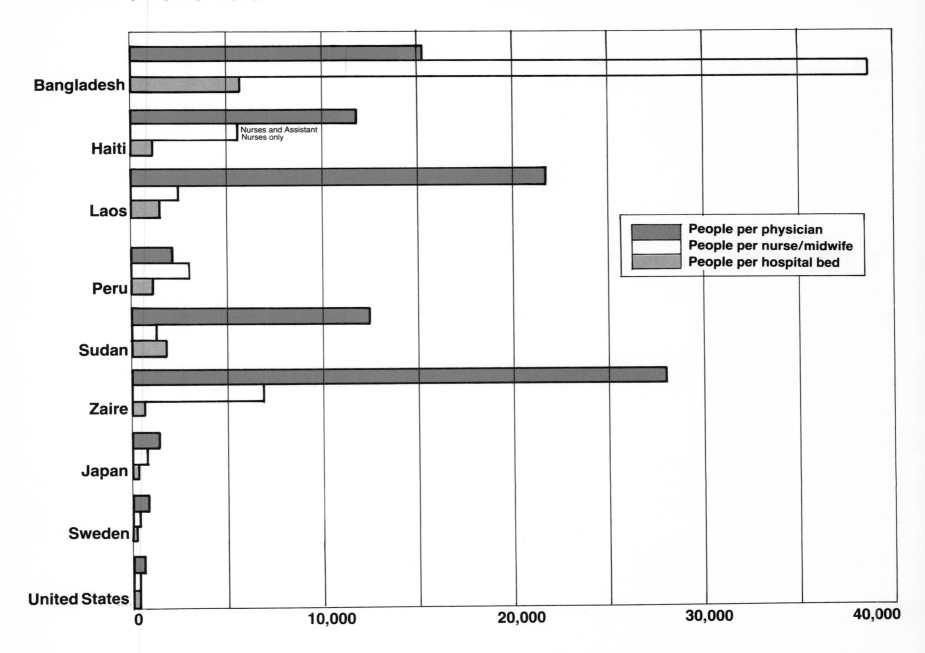

Nurses and Assistant
Nurses only

People per physician
People per nurse/midwife
People per hospital bed

Bangladesh

Haiti

Laos

Peru

Sudan

Zaire

Japan

Sweden

United States

0   10,000   20,000   30,000   40,000

SOURCE: World Health Organization; *Statistics Annual,* 1977

Projected needs for health facilities and personnel in 61 neediest countries,* 1990 and 2000

	1990	2000
Population: (in millions) in poor sector, assumed to be 90 percent of total population	1,095,000	1,415,000
Referral Hospitals	5	7
Rural or Urban Slum Hospitals	22	28
Health Centers	110	142
Community Health Clinics	1,095	1,415
Hospital Beds	4,107	5,307
Physicians	235	304
Nurses	986	1,274
Medium Level Personnel	1,643	2,123
Community Health Workers	6,571	8,491

*Afghanistan, Algeria, Angola, Bangladesh, Benin, Bhutan, Bolivia, Botswana, Burma, Burundi, Cameroon, Central African Empire, Chad, Colombia, Congo, El Salvador, Equitorial Guinea, Ethiopia, Gabon, Gambia, Ghana, Guinea, Guinea Bissau, Haiti, Honduras, India, Indonesia, Ivory Coast, Kampuchea, Kenya, Laos, Lesotho, Liberia, Madagascar, Malawi, Mali, Mauritania, Morocco, Mozambique, Nepal, Niger, Nigeria, Pakistan, Papua New Guinea, Philippines, Portuguese-Timor, Rwanda, Senegal, Sierra Leone, Somalia, Sudan, Swaziland, Tanzania, Togo, Tunisia, Uganda, Upper Volta, Yemen A.R., Yemen P.R., Zaire, Zambia.

These projected needs are based on the assumption that for one million people in the poor sector, the following are required:

- 1,000 community health clinics with 5,000 community health workers

- 100 health centers with 100 physicians, 500 nurses, 500 other medium level personnel and 1,000 community health workers

- 20 rural or urban slum hospitals with 40 physicians, 100 nurses, 500 other medium level personnel and 2,000 beds

- 5 referral hospitals with 75 physicians, 300 nurses, 500 other medium level personnel and 1,750 beds

SOURCES: United Nations Population Division, WP 60; Norbye, *World Development*, February 1974; United Nations, *Demographic Yearbook*, 1973

Ten million children under age five suffer from extreme malnutrition, and an additional 90 million, from moderate malnutrition. Besides increasing vulnerability to disease, malnutrition is in itself a prime cause of infant and child mortality. Of all recorded deaths of infants and children, 50 to 75 percent are caused by a combination of malnutrition and infectious disease. In malnourished children who survive, growth is stunted and many suffer brain damage that can incapacitate them for life.

Widespread malnutrition in less developed countries affects children even before birth. Poorly nourished mothers often suffer fetal deaths and stillbirths or bear children of low birth weight which increases the health hazards of infancy.

After birth, children in many parts of the less developed world do not get enough food or do not get the right food. They develop protein energy malnutrition, a most serious public health problem. The three main forms of protein energy malnutrition are marasmus, or starvation, due to a severe lack of calories, often brought on when an infant is starved in an effort to cure prolonged diarrhea caused by inadequate and unsanitary bottle feeding; kwashiorkor due to severe protein deficiency; and nutritional growth retardation due to inadequate food intake, usually associated with recurrent infections.

In many less developed countries, cultural taboos limit the types of food that are available. Still more often, there is simply not enough of any type of food to feed everyone adequately, and when food is short, children and women are frequently the last to be fed. In Bolivia during the early 1970s, the calorie content of food available on a daily per capita basis was only 78 percent of the level considered by the Food and Agriculture Organization (FAO) of the United Nations as sufficient to maintain "moderate activity;" in Mali the available calories represented 75 percent of that level, and in Upper Volta, 73 percent. At the same time in most developed countries the number of calories available per capita exceeded 120 percent of the level established by FAO as sufficient for "moderate activity." Some children in more developed countries consume too many calories and develop obesity, in itself detrimental to good health.

Even if the number of calories available per capita is adequate, the diets of children may be deficient in proteins, vitamins, and other essential food elements. As noted, severe protein deficiency causes kwashiorkor which often results when a breastfed infant must be weaned on the arrival of another baby and is fed a starchy diet lacking in proteins which leaves the infant vulnerable to infections. Still more common in less developed countries is anemia due to iron deficiency. And every year up to one hundred thousand children, particularly in Southeast Asia, are blinded by xerophthalmia caused by lack of Vitamin A. In its program to deal with malnutrition of children, the World Health Organization is giving special attention to promoting local foods which can meet children's particular needs for proteins and is attempting to remedy Vitamin A deficiency by direct administration of the vitamin and fortification of suitable foods.

Intestinal parasites such as hookworm and tapeworm, common in tropical and semitropical climates of many less developed countries, reduce the absorption of protein and certain vitamins and may cause malnutrition even in a child who has a relatively good diet. Roundworm, associated with overcrowding and poor sanitation, is estimated to affect more than one-half billion people around the world.

Causes and effects of childhood malnutrition, about 1975

Insufficient food	Insufficient quality of food	Food spoilage	Lack of education/ information	Poverty and deprivation	Poor sanitation
•Thirty-seven countries most affected by food shortage have per capita grain production below 1969-71 levels. Thirty-four have a trend of falling per capita grain production.	•A young child's protein needs are proportionately 2½ times as great as an adult's. •For an adequate diet, the 32 poorest countries need to triple their production of meat and fish, and greatly increase production of milk, eggs, fruits, and vegetables.	•In many countries food spoilage runs higher than 30% of total food production. •Overall loss due to pests is about 20% of the world's food supply per year. •Rats, insects, and fungi destroy 33 million tons of food in storage per year.	•Insufficient and poor use of teachers, agricultural extension workers, community development agents. •Illiteracy: 800 million illiterates worldwide. In many countries half the population over 15 is illiterate, and the number is rising. •Non-reliance on breast-feeding. Breast-feeding can provide all that is required in first six months of life. •Unregulated fertility of mothers.	•In some Asian and African countries, daily per capita income is 20-24 U.S. cents. •Mothers, handicapped since early life by nutritional deficiency and environmental hazards, give birth to low weight infants, and are too exhausted to give adequate child care.	•Lack of clean water, safe environment, uncontaminat food and decent living spac •In 91 less developed countries, 71% of the population had no access to clean drinking water (1970); 83% of ru population had no safe drinking water available. •In some parts of the world, women and children spend half their time carrying wat

Stunted physical and mental development	Susceptibility to infectious diseases	Susceptibility to vector-borne diseases	Susceptibility to gastro-intestinal diseases

Early death, serious and permanent damage

•Malnutrition: the biggest single contributor to illness and death among children in the less developed countries where 25% of the children die before age five (a rate 20-40 times higher than in the more developed world).

•Half the deaths of children under five are caused by malnutrition.

•Loss of body fluid and salt depletion from diarrhea leads to debilitation and death.

•Five million children in the less developed countries are killed each year by diphtheria, whooping cough, tetanus, poliomyelitis, measles, and tuberculosis.

•Vitamin A deficiency causes 20-100,000 children to lose their sight each year.

•Water-related diseases kill approximately ten million people a year. The diseases are: water-borne, e.g., cholera, typhoid; water-washed, e.g., typhus, trachoma (a leading cause of blindness in young children); water-based, e.g., guinea worms; plus vector-borne, e.g., malaria; and those related to fecal disposal.

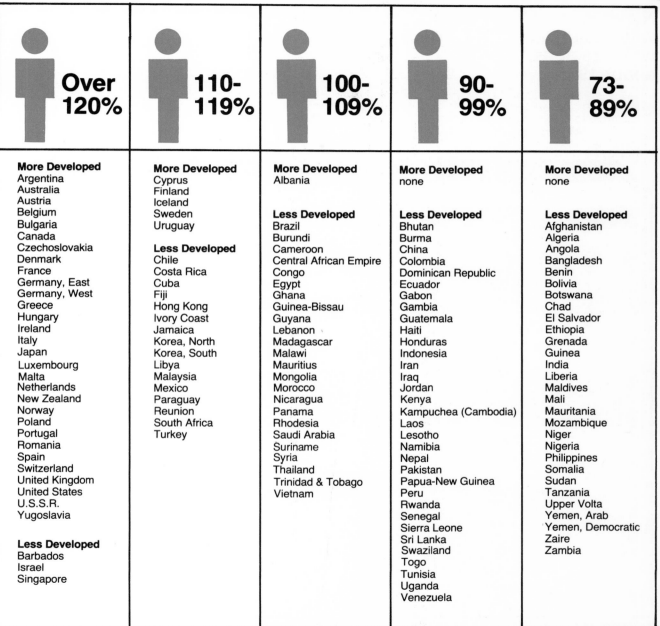

tisfaction of daily per pita calorie requirements country, 1972-1974

he percentages by which the coun-
are classified were prepared by the
d and Agriculture Organization
) of the United Nations based on
estimated per capita calorie supply
od available in each country in
2-1974 divided by the average daily
capita caloric intake which the FAO
ulates as necessary to maintain
derate activity." This takes into
ount the age-sex structure of the
population, climate, average body
ht, and other factors in each
ntry.

Over 120%	110-119%	100-109%	90-99%	73-89%
More Developed	**More Developed**	**More Developed**	**More Developed**	**More Developed**
Argentina	Cyprus	Albania	none	none
Australia	Finland			
Austria	Iceland		**Less Developed**	**Less Developed**
Belgium	Sweden	**Less Developed**	Bhutan	Afghanistan
Bulgaria	Uruguay	Brazil	Burma	Algeria
Canada		Burundi	China	Angola
Czechoslovakia	**Less Developed**	Cameroon	Colombia	Bangladesh
Denmark	Chile	Central African Empire	Dominican Republic	Benin
France	Costa Rica	Congo	Ecuador	Bolivia
Germany, East	Cuba	Egypt	Gabon	Botswana
Germany, West	Fiji	Ghana	Gambia	Chad
Greece	Hong Kong	Guinea-Bissau	Guatemala	El Salvador
Hungary	Ivory Coast	Guyana	Haiti	Ethiopia
Ireland	Jamaica	Lebanon	Honduras	Grenada
Italy	Korea, North	Madagascar	Indonesia	Guinea
Japan	Korea, South	Malawi	Iran	India
Luxembourg	Libya	Mauritius	Iraq	Liberia
Malta	Malaysia	Mongolia	Jordan	Maldives
Netherlands	Mexico	Morocco	Kenya	Mali
New Zealand	Paraguay	Nicaragua	Kampuchea (Cambodia)	Mauritania
Norway	Reunion	Panama	Laos	Mozambique
Poland	South Africa	Rhodesia	Lesotho	Niger
Portugal	Turkey	Saudi Arabia	Namibia	Nigeria
Romania		Suriname	Nepal	Philippines
Spain		Syria	Pakistan	Somalia
Switzerland		Thailand	Papua-New Guinea	Sudan
United Kingdom		Trinidad & Tobago	Peru	Tanzania
United States		Vietnam	Rwanda	Upper Volta
U.S.S.R.			Senegal	Yemen, Arab
Yugoslavia			Sierra Leone	Yemen, Democratic
			Sri Lanka	Zaire
			Swaziland	Zambia
Less Developed			Togo	
Barbados			Tunisia	
Israel			Uganda	
Singapore			Venezuela	

SOURCE: Food and Agriculture Organization of the United Nations, *Fourth World Food Survey*, 1977

Number of children under age 15 with insufficient food energy levels, world regions, about 1975

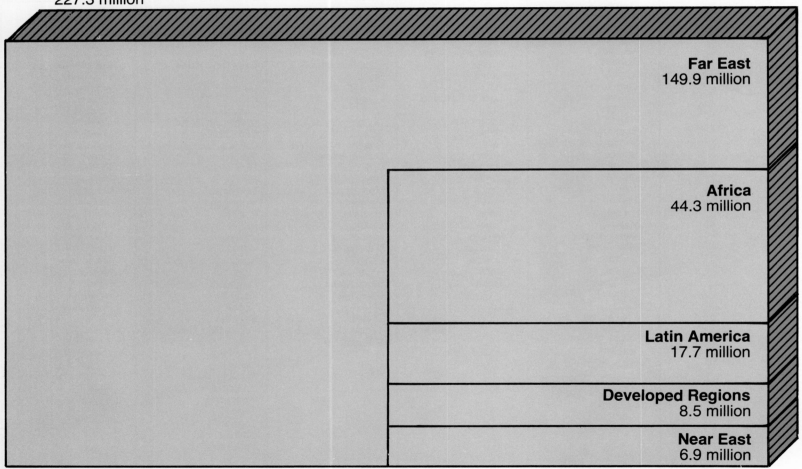

World Total*
227.3 million

Far East
149.9 million

Africa
44.3 million

Latin America
17.7 million

Developed Regions
8.5 million

Near East
6.9 million

*Excluding centrally planned economies

The Near East includes Greece, Egypt, and the Asian countries of Bahrain, Cyprus, Iran, Iraq, Israel, Jordan, Kuwait, Lebanon, Oman, Qatar, Saudi Arabia, Syria, Turkey, United Arab Emirates, Yemen, and Democratic Yemen. The Far East includes all other Asian countries and Oceania, except for Australia and New Zealand.

SOURCE: Adapted from Food and Agriculture Organization estimate (1970) that percentages of country populations below the lower limit of food energy levels are: More developed regions, 3%; Latin America, 13%; Far East, 30%; Near East, 18%; Africa, 25%

ncipal nutritional deficiency diseases
the world affecting children

ase	What are they – how to detect them	Foods that prevent the disease
emia	Insufficient hemoglobin (the substance which transports oxygen in the blood). Usually caused by iron deficiency. Main symptoms: pallor of skin and mucous membranes, general fatigue, breathlessness after exertion, palpitation, loss of appetite (anorexia), indigestion (dyspepsia).	all kinds of meat, but especially liver fruits, especially citrus fruits, guava, mango, pineapple, berries green vegetables
demic oiter	Enlargement of the thyroid gland resulting from iodine deficiency. Main symptoms: deformity of the neck by enlarged thyroid gland. Mental retardation and deaf-mutism may occur in children born to mother with goiter.	iodized salt Endemic goiter has been eliminated in areas where the salt is iodized. sea foods, such as fish, shellfish and algae
ashiorkor	Severe protein deficiency. Main symptoms: swelling (edema), apathy and irritability, "flaky-paint" skin, sparse, straight and depigmented hair, muscle weakness and diarrhea.	milk and cheese meats and fish eggs beans, peas and lentils groundnuts
arasmus	Severe calorie deficiency. Main symptoms: growth retardation, wasting, no subcutaneous fat, atrophied muscles – "all skin and bone." The severe wasting of children with this disease makes them look like very old people.	breast milk for infants cereals, such as rice, wheat or maize roots and tubers (potatoes, yams or cassava) fats and oils
rophthalmia	Severe Vitamin A deficiency. Main symptoms: dryness of the eyes (xerosis), night-blindness (nyctalopia), corneal ulcerations, leading to blindness.	whole milk, butter and cheese yolk of eggs and liver vegetables, especially carrots and "greens" yellow fruits, such as mango and papaya red palm oil

CE: World Health Organization, *World Health,* May 1977

Food energy requirements of children and adolescents by age

Age (years)	Body Weight (kg.)	Calories per person per day
Children		
0-1	7.3	820
1-3	13.4	1,360
4-6	20.2	1,830
7-9	28.1	2,190
Male Adolescents		
10-12	36.9	2,600
13-15	51.3	2,900
16-19	62.9	3,070
Female Adolescents		
10-12	38.0	2,350
13-15	49.9	2,490
16-19	54.4	2,310

SOURCE: Report of a joint Food and Agriculture Organization/World Health Organization committee, 1973

Percentages of inhabitants served by sewerage facilities, selected less developed countries, about 1970

Regions	Coverage (% inhabitants of each region)	Urban			Rural with adequate disposal	Percent of total population with sewage disposal
		Connected to public sewerage system	Household system	Total		
Total 58 less developed countries	59	28.1	44.2	72.3	7.6	24.5
of which:						
22 in Africa	43	18.2	32.2	50.4	14.3	21.4
17 in Latin America	94	34.5	28.4	62.9	20.1	43.1
17 in Asia	51	25.8	55.5	81.3	4.9	20.6
2 in Oceania	3	13.7	56.1	69.8	90.9	84.1

The countries included in this table are:
Africa: Algeria, Benin, Burundi, Central African Empire, Chad, Ethiopia, Guinea, Ivory Coast, Kenya, Liberia, Libyan Arab Republic, Madagascar, Mali, Mauritania, Mauritius, Morocco, Niger, Tunisia, Uganda, Upper Volta, Zaire, Zambia.
Latin America: Bolivia, Brazil, Colombia, Costa Rica, Dominican Republic, Ecuador, El Salvador, Guatemala, Guyana, Haiti, Honduras, Jamaica, Mexico, Nicaragua, Panama, Peru, Venezuela.
Asia: Afghanistan, Bangladesh, Burma, Indonesia, Iran, Iraq, Kampuchea, Laos, Malaysia, Nepal, Philippines, Saudi Arabia, Singapore, South Korea, South Vietnam, Sri Lanka, Thailand.
Oceania: Fiji and Western Samoa.

SOURCE: World Health Organization, *Statistics Report,* November 1973

sanitation

Lack of adequate sewer systems and lack of safe, water result in increased ease and high death rates millions of the world's chil Drinking and playing in co taminated water causes diarrheal and other intestir diseases.

Fewer than 35 percent people in the less develop countries have reasonable access to satisfactory drin water or hygienic waste di posal.

The World Health Orgar tion estimates that up to 8 percent of the world's dise are traceable to contamina water.

**ldren in rural populations
hout access to safe water,
out 1975**
(imates in millions)

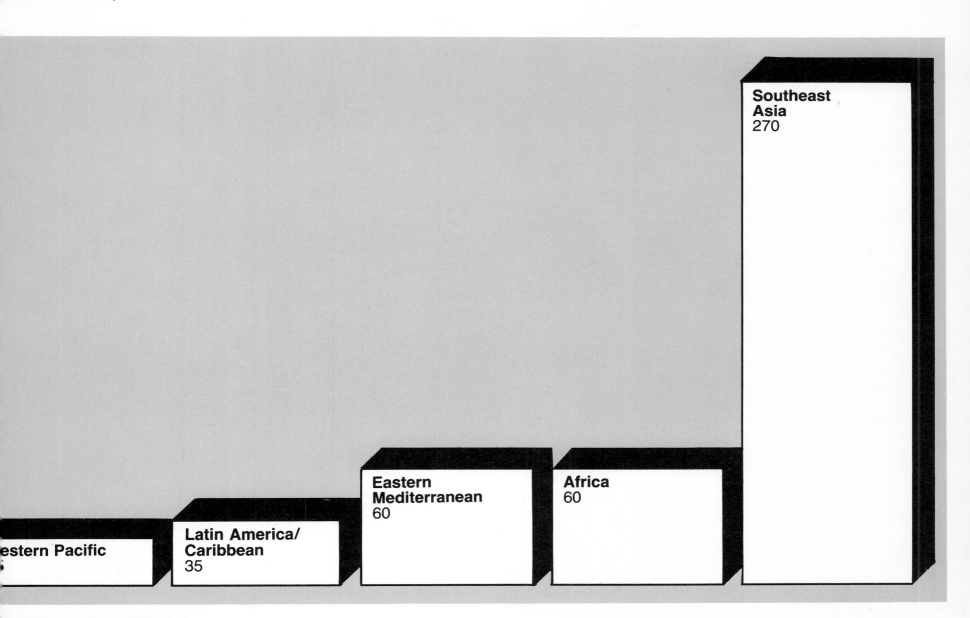

Southeast
Asia
270

Eastern
Mediterranean
60

Africa
60

Latin America/
Caribbean
35

estern Pacific

CE: UNICEF, *Children, Water and UNICEF,* undated

World summary of handicapped children, about 1975

Handicaps ranging from minor mental disturbances to major physical disabilities such as blindness represent serious obstacles to a child's development. They affect 15-20% of the world's children, with 5% suffering severe handicaps. These children are the victims of birth defects, crippling diseases, and impairments caused by the environment. They require special care, services, and education.

In the less developed regions, the proportion of handicapped children is higher due to deprivation caused by poverty. Three percent of their children under five suffer severe protein/calorie malnutrition (kwashiorkor or marasmus), and 8-10% in some regions have eye troubles due to vitamin A deficiency. In the less developed countries 50-60 million children could benefit from special education, and 5 million are too handicapped to benefit from normal education. More specifically:

Less developed regions
- In Bangladesh, there are 50,000 blind children in need of surgery.
- In India (1966), 1.4-1.8 million children were mentally retarded.
- In Tanzania (1968), 20-25,000 children suffered from leprosy, and 20-30,000 from effects of poliomyelitis.

More developed regions
- In West Germany, 60,000+ children per year are born with a physical or mental disability that needs special attention. There are 500,500 handicapped children of school age.
- In France, there are 938,000 handicapped children.
- In Turkey, 761,272 children are handicapped. This is 15% of all Turkish children.

United States

Of 48.5 million children of school age (6-17), 12% are rated as handicapped.

Handicapped	Number (in thousands)
Blind (Visually impaired)	42.8
Deaf (hard of hearing)	246.0
Crippled	213.9
Speech-impaired	1,497.1
Emotionally disturbed	855.5
Mentally retarded	983.8
Learning disabled	1,283.2
Multihandicapped	25.7
Handicapped children in private schools	516.0
TOTAL	5,664.0

SOURCES: United Nations Department of Economic and Social Affairs, ST/ESA/47, 1976; U.S. News and World Report, February 27, 1978

the handicapp

Physically and mentally handicapped children are in need of special care, but th poorest countries lack finan and human resources to de with these problems.

ual infant deaths per 1000 live births (versus 22
1000 in more developed regions): **113**

ll deaths in children under five, less developed
s account for: **90%**

ber of children killed each year by diphtheria,
oping cough, tetanus, poliomyelitis, measles,
rculosis: **5 million**

t of vaccine for immunizing one child from major
g diseases (over 90% of children in the more
eloped countries are so immunized): **U.S. $0.675**

ber of children disabled through brain damage,
lysis, stunted growth, deafness, blindness: **10 million**

Proportion of health expenditure allocated to highly
sophisticated, disease-oriented, institutional care of
individual patients (leaving large numbers under-
served, if at all): **75% (often)**

Doctors living in big cities (whereas 80% or more of
the population live in rural areas): **80%**

Of 105 million children born each year in the less
developed countries, those ever seen by health
workers: **10%**
(less than)

Rural population living within walking distance of a **15%**
health facility of any kind: **(less than)**

Proportion of health needs in the villages that can
be dealt with by auxiliary health workers: **85%**

E: UNICEF, *Health Facts*, 1978

education

Millions of children have no opportunity to attend school. In some less developed countries, as many as nine of every ten children in the rural areas grow up unable to read or write. Although the proportion of children enrolled in school has been increasing in the less developed countries, less than two thirds (62 percent) of those in the primary school ages of 6-11 were enrolled in 1975 compared to 94 percent in the more developed regions as a whole. And about half of those who do enter school drop out before completing the minimum four or five years necessary to achieve and retain basic literacy.

Girls in the less developed countries are far less likely to be in school than boys. In 1975, just over half (53 percent) of girls aged 6-11 were in school in the less developed countries as a whole, compared to 70 percent of boys of this age. At the secondary school level – ages 12-17 – the proportions were 28 percent for girls and 42 percent for boys. By contrast, in the more developed regions, enrollment ratios were equal for boys and girls in the primary school ages – 94 percent. And at the secondary school level, relatively more girls were enrolled than boys – 85 versus 84 percent.

The low school enrollment of girls in the less developed countries reinforces the circle of educational deprivation, for when these girls become mothers they are less able to help their children become literate. It is estimated that two thirds of the world's 800 million illiterate adults in 1975 were women.

As yet, there are not enough teachers in the less developed regions. The number of teachers is growing rapidly, but the school-age population is growing even more rapidly. Despite an increase of four million primary-school teachers in the less developed countries between 1960 and 1975, the ratio of children to teacher is high. For example, in 1975, in Afghanistan, there were 258 school-age (5-19)children per teacher; in India, there were 80 school-age children per teacher. By comparison, in New Zealand, there were 28 children per teacher; and in the Netherlands, 35.

Percent of children aged 6-11 and 12-17 enrolled in school, more developed and less developed regions, 1975

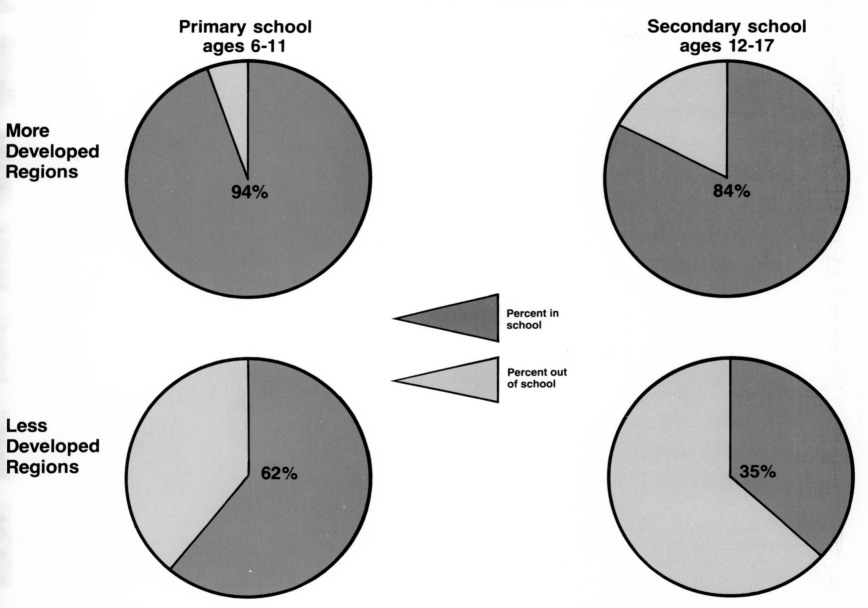

**Primary school
ages 6-11**

**Secondary school
ages 12-17**

**More
Developed
Regions**

94%

84%

Percent in
school

Percent out
of school

**Less
Developed
Regions**

62%

35%

SOURCE: UNESCO Office of Statistics

Percent of boys and girls aged 6-11 and 12-17 enrolled in school, more developed and less developed regions, 1960-2000

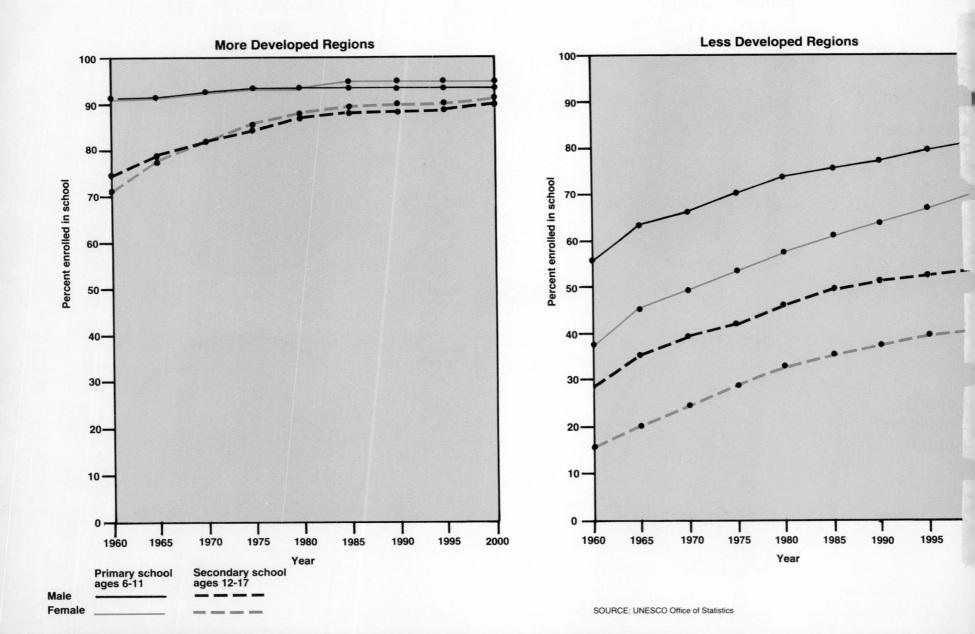

More Developed Regions

Less Developed Regions

Percent enrolled in school

Year

Primary school
ages 6-11

Secondary school
ages 12-17

Male

Female

SOURCE: UNESCO Office of Statistics

Percent of boys and girls aged 6-11 and 12-17 enrolled in school, selected countries, 1975

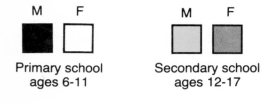

M   F   M   F

Primary school   Secondary school
ages 6-11   ages 12-17

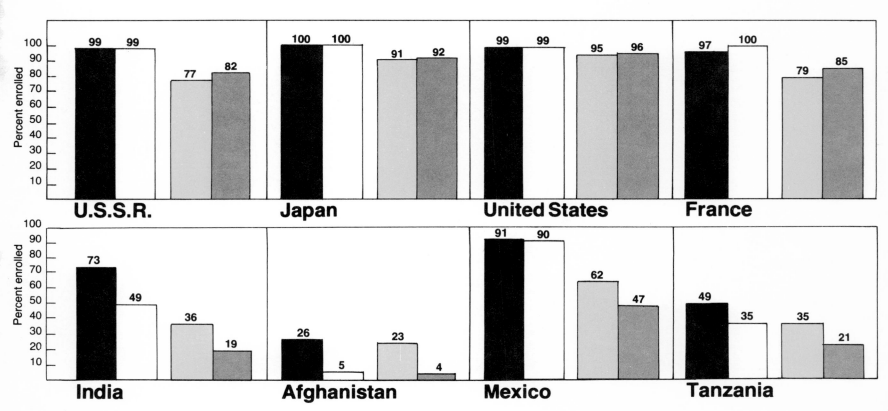

SOURCE: Population Reference Bureau, *World's Children Data Sheet*, 1979

Number of pupils enrolled in school at all levels, world, more developed and less developed regions, 1950-1974

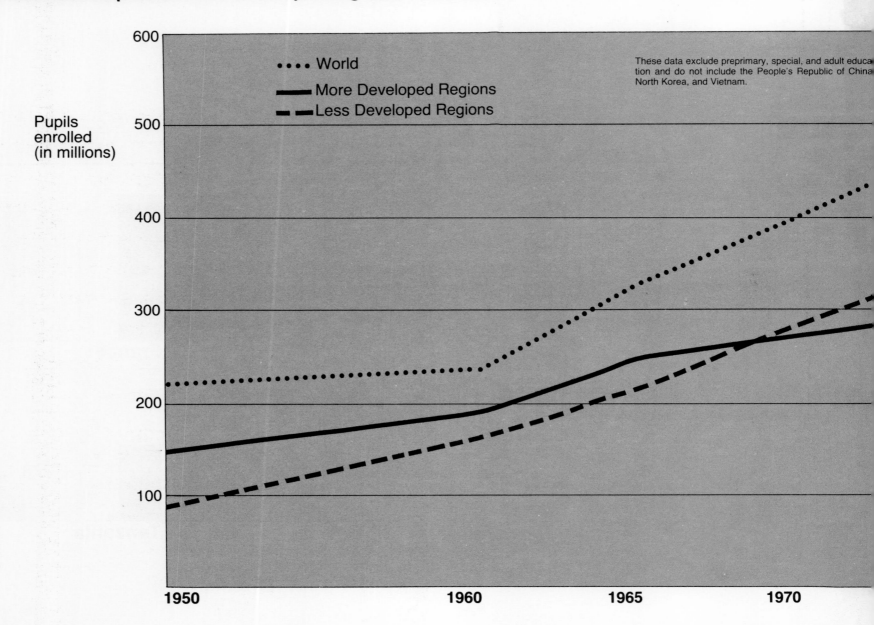

Pupils enrolled (in millions)

These data exclude preprimary, special, and adult education and do not include the People's Republic of China, North Korea, and Vietnam.

- •••• World
- ▬▬ More Developed Regions
- ▬ ▬ Less Developed Regions

SOURCE: UNESCO, *Statistical Yearbook*, 1972, 1976

s at which education is compulsory and age at which ondary education begins, selected countries, about 1975

is chart illustrates the disparities that in different countries' regulations on pulsory education and which age ps they include at the various levels ucation. The UNESCO *Statistical book,* 1975, points out that: "In many tries and territories where the urgent em is to provide sufficient schools for ildren, the existence of compulsory ol laws may be only of academic in- t since almost all such regulations pt a child from attending if there is no ble school within reasonable dis- of home."

Ages at which education is compulsory

Age at which secondary education begins

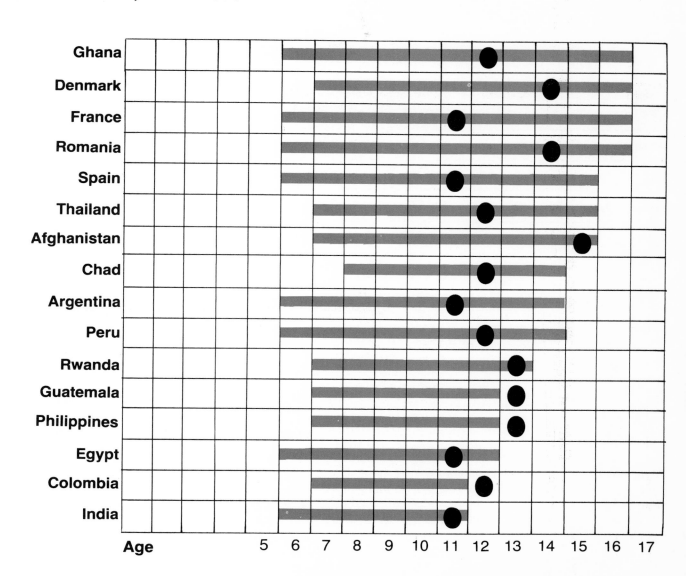

UNESCO, *Statistical Yearbook*, 1975

Extent of preprimary education* for comparable numbers of people in selected countries of Africa, Asia, Latin America and Europe, about 1975

Region	Total 1975 pop. of selected countries (in millions)	Teaching staff (in thousands)	Pupils enrolled (in thousands)
Africa	76.5	2.6	100.5
Asia	73.3	10.7	316.0
Latin America	73.9	13.5	410.1
Europe	73.6	82.8	1977.9

Countries selected:
Africa: Egypt (1973), Ghana (1972), Zaire (1972), Angola (1972), Sudan (1971)
Asia: Hong Kong (1973), Iraq (1974), Malaysia (1973), Mongolia (1974), Philippines (1972)
Latin America: Colombia (1973), Peru (1973), Uruguay (1973), Venezuela (1973), Ecuador (1973), Chile (1974)
Europe: Austria (1973), Bulgaria (1973), Netherlands (1973), Spain (1973), Sweden (1972)

*Preprimary education consists of kindergartens and nursery schools as well as infant classes attached to schools at higher levels.

In the first few years of life, a child's capacity to learn develops more rapidly than at any other comparable life stage. Unfortunately, these years are least provided for in formal education, especially in less developed countries which are hard pressed to provide education for older children.

SOURCE: United Nations Population Division, WP 60; UNESCO, *Statistical Yearbook*, 1975

Number of teachers at all levels, world, more developed and less developed regions 1950-1974

Numbers of teachers have been increasing more rapidly in less developed countries than in more developed regions. However, the school-age population has been growing even faster so that the numbers of children to be served by each teacher are still very large.

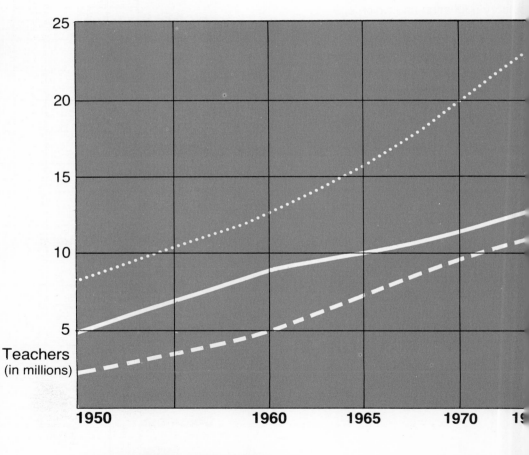

More Developed Regions
Less Developed Regions
World*

*Excluding People's Republic of Cl North Korea, and Vietnam.

SOURCE: UNESCO, *Statistical Yearbook*, 1

Percent of school-age population (5-19) enrolled in school and number of school-age children per teacher, selected countries, 1975

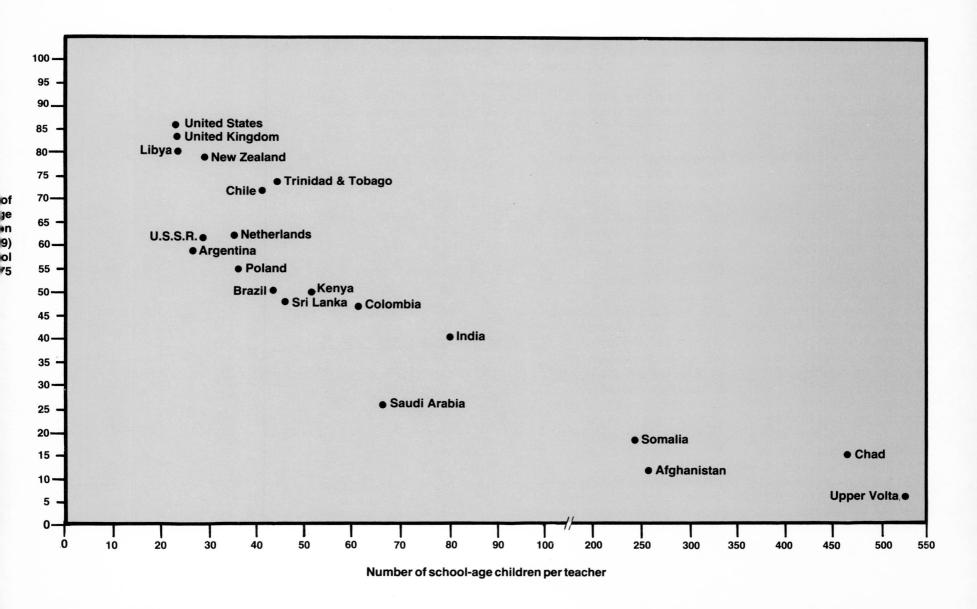

Number of school-age children per teacher

SOURCE: Ruth Leger Sivard, *World Military and Social Expenditures*, 1978

employment

Although children below the age of 15 are not usually considered part of the work force, large numbers of them in the less developed world do work. In 1975, some 55 million children under age 15 were at work around the world, according to the International Labor Organization (ILO). There were 30.5 million in South Asia; 9.9 million in East Asia; 9.6 million in Africa; 3.3 million in Latin America; and 1.3 million in all the other generally more developed countries.

These estimates refer only to fulltime child workers and represent only the "tip of the iceberg" because children are not usually covered in statistical surveys of the labor force. Even so, the estimates for some countries are very high. For example, in 1975, 36 percent of boys and 24 percent of girls aged 10-14 were working fulltime in Tanzania; in Brazil the figures were 16 percent for boys and 6 percent for girls; and in Thailand, 23 percent for boys and 28 percent for girls. The ILO projects a decline in the number of child workers to about 37 million in the year 2000 as countries become more developed and more children can be accommodated in school.

Most children in the ILO statistics for 1975 were working without pay to supply the extra hands needed for their families' survival – mainly in rural areas. Both boys and girls help in the fields and tend animals; girls help prepare food, care for younger children, and carry water. Other children are paid for working in small factories, in cottage industries such as rug-making, in the fields, and in domestic service, but their wages are usually far below those of adults.

Children in paid employment face increasing competition for their jobs from older children. They also face the likelihood of unemployment as they themselves grow older. Unemployment and underemployment are currently far higher among young would-be workers aged 15-24 than among older adults in both less and more developed countries.

For children in the less developed countries, the prospects for employment as they reach full adulthood are even bleaker. Already in 1978 some 300 to 500 million members of the world's labor force were out of work, mainly in the less developed countries. And with the large numbers of children due to enter the working ages in the last two decades of the twentieth century, the world's labor force will rise from 1.6 billion in 1975 to 2.5 billion in the year 2000 – an increase of 900 million in this quarter-century.

Number of children under age 15 in the labor force, world regions, 1975 and 2000

(in millions)

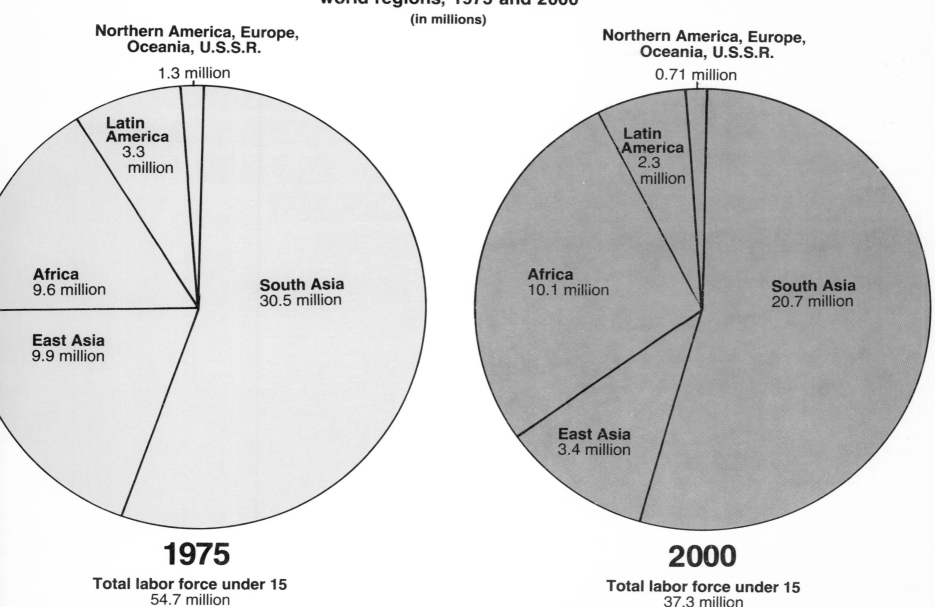

Northern America, Europe, Oceania, U.S.S.R.
1.3 million

Latin America
3.3 million

Africa
9.6 million

East Asia
9.9 million

South Asia
30.5 million

1975

Total labor force under 15
54.7 million

Northern America, Europe, Oceania, U.S.S.R.
0.71 million

Latin America
2.3 million

Africa
10.1 million

East Asia
3.4 million

South Asia
20.7 million

2000

Total labor force under 15
37.3 million

E: International Labor Office, *Labor Force Estimates and Projections, 1950-2000*, 1977

Percent of children aged 10-14 in the labor force, selected countries, 1975

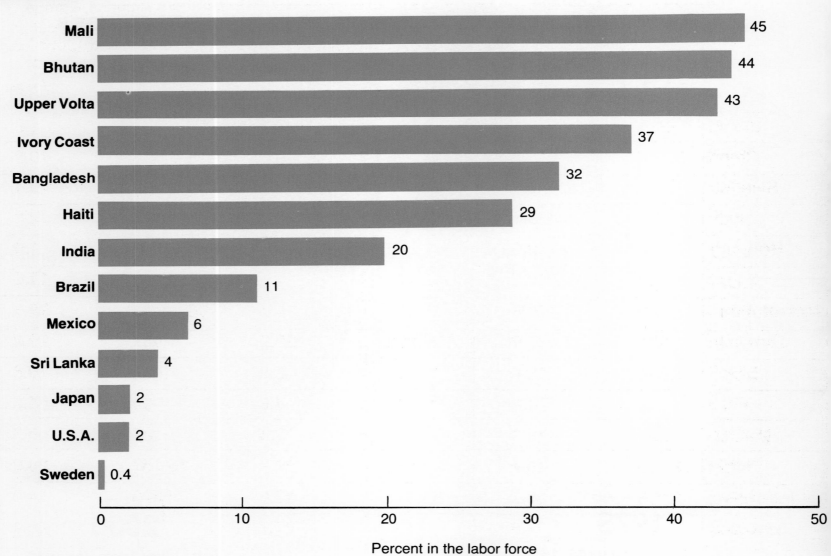

Percent in the labor force

SOURCE: International Labor Office; *Labor Force Estimates and Projections, 1950-2000*, 1977

Number and percent of boys and girls aged 10-14 in the labor force, selected countries, 1975

	Boys		Girls		Total	
	In the labor force		In the labor force		In the labor force	
	Number (in thousands)	Percent	Number (in thousands)	Percent	Number (in thousands)	Percent
U.S.A.	221	2.1	106	1.1	327	1.6
China	5,397	12.2	4,128	9.6	9,525	10.9
Sweden	2	0.6	1	0.3	3	0.4
Italy	70	3.1	44	2.0	114	2.6
Hungary	2	0.6	4	1.3	6	1.0
Egypt	426	18.2	101	4.5	527	11.5
Mozambique	220	41.8	77	14.5	297	28.1
Tanzania	334	35.9	223	23.9	557	29.9
Brazil	1,054	15.8	382	5.8	1,436	10.8
Peru	44	4.6	40	4.3	84	4.5
Mexico	390	10.0	91	2.4	481	6.3
India	7,620	19.4	7,537	20.7	15,157	20.0
Indonesia	1,425	16.5	1,048	12.5	2,473	14.5
Thailand	623	23.0	730	27.7	1,353	25.4

SOURCE: International Labor Organization, *Labor Force Estimates and Projections, 1950-2000,* 1977

**Employment and unemployment
among adults and youth
aged 15-24,
selected more developed countries,
1976**

Adult unemployment:
8.8 million
Adult unemployment rate:
3.6%

Youth unemployment:
6.9 million
**Youth unemployment
rate: 10.7%**

Adult employment:
236.8 million

Youth employment:
57.6 million

Countries included:

Australia	Japan
Austria	Luxembourg
Belgium	Netherlands
Canada	New Zealand
Denmark	Norway
Finland	Portugal
France	Spain
Germany	Sweden
Greece	Switzerland
Iceland	United Kingdom
Ireland	United States
Italy	

Total labor force:
310.1 million

Ratio of youth to adult unemployment rate:
3.0

Youth labor force
64.5 million

Total adult labor f
245.6 million

SOURCE: *OECD Observer*, January 1978

Growth of world labor force, 1750-2000

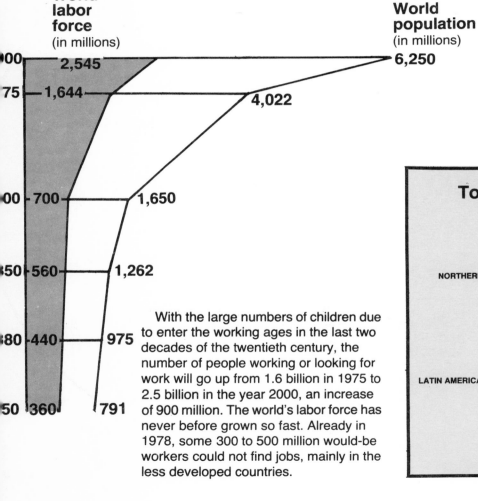

World labor force
(in millions)

World population
(in millions)

'00	2,545	6,250
'75	1,644	4,022
'00	700	1,650
'50	560	1,262
'80	440	975
'50	360	791

With the large numbers of children due to enter the working ages in the last two decades of the twentieth century, the number of people working or looking for work will go up from 1.6 billion in 1975 to 2.5 billion in the year 2000, an increase of 900 million. The world's labor force has never before grown so fast. Already in 1978, some 300 to 500 million would-be workers could not find jobs, mainly in the less developed countries.

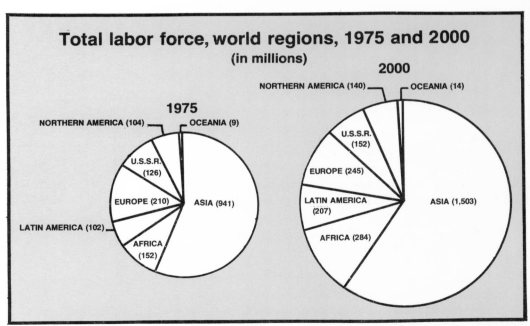

Total labor force, world regions, 1975 and 2000
(in millions)

1975

NORTHERN AMERICA (104)
OCEANIA (9)
U.S.S.R. (126)
EUROPE (210)
ASIA (941)
LATIN AMERICA (102)
AFRICA (152)

2000

NORTHERN AMERICA (140)
OCEANIA (14)
U.S.S.R. (152)
EUROPE (245)
LATIN AMERICA (207)
ASIA (1,503)
AFRICA (284)

S: Ypsilantis, *ILO Review*, May/June 1974; International Labor Office, *Labor Force Estimates and Projections, 1950-2000*, 1977